MY NAPTOWN MEMORIES

*One Boy's Life Growing Up In Indianapolis
In The 1930s & 1940s*

RAYMOND M. FEATHERSTONE JR.

iUniverse, Inc.
New York   Bloomington

MY NAPTOWN MEMORIES
One Boy's Life Growing Up In Indianapolis-1930s & 1940s

iUniverse books may be ordered through booksellers or by contacting:

iUniverse
1663 Liberty Drive
Bloomington, IN 47403
www.iuniverse.com
1-800-Authors (1-800-288-4677)

Because of the dynamic nature of the Internet, any Web addresses or links contained in this book may have changed since publication and may no longer be valid. The views expressed in this work are solely those of the author and do not necessarily reflect the views of the publisher, and the publisher hereby disclaims any responsibility for them.

ISBN: 978-1-4401-1488-5 (sc)
ISBN: 978-1-4401-1489-2 (ebk)

Printed in the United States of America

iUniverse rev. date: 02/10/2009

DEDICATION

This book is dedicated to my long-time best friend, Richard C. Rhude, who was the emotionally older, wiser brother I never had. His was the stabilizing influence in my life throughout those youthful years. We shared many of the same experiences from attending kindergarten through high school together, palling around after school, working as teenagers in various jobs, later dating some of the same girls, to joining the same college fraternity. His sage advice no doubt kept me out of many scrapes and squabbles. This is a belated thank you.

DICK RHUDE AT THE INDIANA UNIVERSITY
PHI SIGMA KAPPA FRATERNITY HOUSE IN 1952

Contents

Acknowledgments

The author would like to thank the following people for their help in making this book possible: Joe Young for his skill in producing the finished photos, and the Indianapolis Motor Speedway and the Indianapolis Star for their permission to use photographs from their archives. Also, thanks to all the people I met while growing up who added seasoning to this story. Finally, thanks to my wife Emily for her support, understanding, and encouragement in this sometimes tedious but enjoyable undertaking.

Introduction

The following narrative is all about what it was like growing up during the Great Depression and World War II on the north side of Indianapolis near the village of Broad Ripple. Growing up then was like no other time in our country's history. Within a fifteen-year period America experienced its greatest economic collapse and the most deadly war. At the height of the Great Depression, twenty-five percent of the work force was without a job. That economic stagnation lasted from 1929 to the prelude of our entry into WW II in 1941. By the end of the war in September 1945, the U.S. had twelve million men and women in uniform and had suffered over one million casualties. Yet we children growing up in a typical middle class neighborhood were somehow shielded from most of the negative consequences associated with those hard and troubled times.

I have tried to describe the 1930s and 1940s as a youngster would have done at the time, including words and phrases as well as fads and fashions that were popular. There are several references to national and local events and people and places that touched my young life. After reading this narrative, you might consider if growing up today is really as much fun as as it was then. Back then Indianapolis had the nickname Naptown. Maybe it wasn't such a pejorative term after all. That is, if you were growing up here at the time.

Fortunately changes came slowly for many of us in the 1930s and 1940s. For example, from the time I was a year old until I graduated from grade school there was only one U.S. president, Franklin Delano Roosevelt. There was only one great heavyweight boxing champion, Joe Louis, known as the Brown Bomber. Joe defended his title twenty-five times between 1937 and 1948.

My family, consisting of my father, mother, sister Mary Ellen and me, lived in the same house on Park Avenue throughout my elementary and high school years. Our neighbors seldom changed since few people moved in those days. The retail shops in our local neighborhood stayed practically unchanged. I graduated from the eighth grade with most of the same children I started with in the first grade. Dad worked all those years for the same company, Westinghouse Electric Corporation. Our 1933 Buick stayed with us all those years until it was traded in for a seven-year-newer model in 1947. Even our pet Cocker Spaniel "Skippy" was part of the family during my twelve years in elementary and high school.

The Early Years In Chicago

It all started when my grandfather and his three brothers inherited a large downtown Chicago iron foundry, Featherstone and Sons, from their father in the late 1880s. After my great grandfather's death the business continued in operation for just a few years. Due to the severe economic recession at the time and the mismanagement of the firm by the brothers, the company went bankrupt in the early 1890s. During that period and for many years more my grandparents and family lived the good life in a fifteen room, three-story limestone mansion on the near north side of Chicago. Dad remembered when he was a young child his family had several servants in the home. My grandparents continued to live in the grand style long after their main source of income from the foundry had dried up.

While my grandfather George Featherstone was still in the money, he purchased a four acre lake front plot on Brown's Lake near Burlington, Wisconsin. There he had a summer home and carriage house constructed for my grandmother as a wedding gift when they were married in 1889. This became the summer retreat for the families of my Dad and his two brothers for the next seventy years.

THE FEATHERSTONES AT BROWN'S LAKE
DAD–BACK ROW ON LEFT SIDE

In the early 1900s money became so scarce that my grandparents reluctantly decided to rent out the first floor of their Chicago mansion. To convert the first floor into a separate apartment, it was walled off from the stairwell and an interior entry door was constructed for the first floor rental unit. In this manner the outside of the house still looked like a one family dwelling and no neighbors were the wiser. Nothing like keeping up appearances!

An example of my grandparents' mindset was their comment when my uncle told them that he hoped to study law. Their response was "Featherstone's don't become attorneys, we hire them as needed." Fortunately my uncle followed his dream to work in the legal profession and retired many years later as an Illinois assistant state attorney.

Dad's bachelor years were somewhat reminiscent of the plot of the popular British drama series televised in the early 1970's, *Upstairs-Downstairs*, in which the son of the wealthy upstairs family romanced one of the downstairs servants. However in our family Dad, whose parents had several servants at the time, went out of the mansion to find and romance Mom whose parents were servants in another part of Chicago.

Unlike Dad's side of the family who had emigrated from England in the early 1800s, Mom's parents, John and Frances Bodevin, emigrated from Luxembourg in the 1880s. The severe economic downturn in the United States at the time, their lack of education and work experience, and their faulty English prevented my grandparents from finding employment except as servants. My grandfather was hired by the ritzy Chicago Club as a chauffeur, first with horse and carriage and later a large phaeton automobile. My grandmother found employment throughout the Chicago area as a housekeeper for wealthy families. In the early 1900s my grandparents were hired to manage a large house with stables and race track on a small private lake in Eagle, Wisconsin, known as Minnehaha Springs. The property was owned by a wealthy Milwaukee businessman known as the "Salt King" who vacationed at the lake place from time to time.

THE BODEVINS AT MINNEHAHA SPRINGS
MOM–SECOND FROM LEFT

My parents brought these differing backgrounds with them when they first met while working at Stebbins Hardware Company in downtown Chicago after the end of World War I. By the time of their wedding in 1926 Dad worked for Westinghouse Electric at the Merchandise Mart. Dad's parents chose not to attend the wedding ceremony as they felt that he had married beneath his station.

Family Life In Indianapolis

In 1927 Dad was promoted to office manager by Westinghouse and transferred from Chicago to the downtown Indianapolis sales office. My parents' first Indianapolis residence was a north side apartment where my older sister Mary Ellen was born in 1929. A short time later the family moved to a small rental bungalow in the 5500 block of north Carrollton Avenue, eight blocks south of the village of Broad Ripple, where I was born in 1931.

Broad Ripple Village began as two separate communities along what was then called the Central Canal. By 1837 Jacob Coil had mapped the town of Broad Ripple on the north side of the canal. Soon thereafter James and Adam Nelson established the town of Wellington on the south side of the canal. In 1884 the two communities came together and incorporated as Broad Ripple with about one hundred and fifty residents. A few small businesses sprang up to serve the canal laborers and travelers coming by boat from Indianapolis. Mules that were guided along the canal towpaths powered the boats. In 1886, Broad Ripple High School was opened and it has remained a viable educational institution with many well-known graduates over the years, including television talk show host David Letterman.

A housing boom in the early 1900s resulted in the construction of mostly smaller bungalows throughout the area. By then, Broad Ripple had become a summer retreat for Indianapolis, thanks to the nearby White River and White City Amusement Park which opened in 1906. A favorite summertime activity was dining and dancing on the steamers while cruising White River. The local population growth and influx of tourists encouraged merchants to open retail shops along the streetcar and interurban lines. In 1922, the city of Indianapolis annexed the village of Broad Ripple and by the 1930s it had become a major suburban shopping center. In 1945 Indianapolis acquired the sixty-acre private Broad Ripple Amusement Park. Soon thereafter the rides were sold or demolished and the site became a public park.

In 1932 when I was one year old, our family moved to a second small rental bungalow just two blocks away. We stayed there for six years until we moved nearby into our own two story house at 54th and

Park Avenue. Our two Carrollton Avenue houses, both built in the 1920s, had the usual bungalow layout for two-bedroom houses. The walk-through front living room was connected to a dining room and rear eat-in kitchen on one side of the house. A front and rear bedroom with a bathroom connected by a side hallway made up the other half of the bungalow. The total living area of our one-story rental houses was about nine hundred square feet. We never thought of them as small houses at the time.

Similar bungalows were constructed throughout Indianapolis during the 1920s housing boom. In fact the bungalow style house was so popular that a street near our Carrollton bungalow was named Bungalow Court. Just one block long, it is perhaps the shortest street in the city. By 1937, bungalow style houses had become so popular in Indianapolis that a new five-room brick house in the 5300 block of Cornelius Avenue was promoted by the builder as being constructed on the "street of bungalows."

As was often true with bungalows, our house had a wide front porch and a single car garage fronting on the alley. Those small bungalows usually had a full basement, which came in handy for playing indoors on rainy days, and had room for Dad's workbench and a fruit cellar. There was a corner for Mom's wash tub and a clothesline for drying laundry in bad weather. In those days there were no laundromats and few home washing machines or dryers. Consequently Mom spent many hours at the laundry tub, scrubbing wet soapy clothes, linens, and bedding on a washboard. After rinsing them, she fed the wet clothes through a hand-cranked wringer to squeeze out most of the water. If it was a warm dry day, she carried the damp clothes outside to hang on a clothesline. I still remember the fresh airy smell of just-washed clothing dried outside.

My parents had traditional roles of father and mother. That is Dad was the sole breadwinner, while Mom spent most of her day at home taking care of the house and us children. As far as we knew Dad made almost all of the decisions ranging from where we lived to where we went on a Sunday drive. Surprisingly I never heard a single negative comment or argument between my parents. If there were any heated discussions, they must have taken place behind closed doors after my sister Mary Ellen and I were in bed. Mom's primary work station was the kitchen. During the Great Depression Mom was a traditional-ist when it came to cooking. She seldom strayed away from popular American food such as meat loaf, hot dogs, fried chicken, canned veg-etables, and Jell-O salad unless company was coming for dinner. As far as ethnic food was concerned, her idea of eating Italian was to roll hamburger into little balls and put the cooked meat into a casserole dish along with a large can of Franco-American spaghetti sprinkled with Kraft's Parmesan cheese to give it that real Italian flavor. For a Hungarian dinner she mixed the cooked hamburger meat with po-tatoes and cabbage, added a gravy sauce, sprinkled the mixture with paprika, and called it Hungarian goulash.

In late summer, my sister and I picked ripe fruit from the trees in our back yard for immediate eating or canning by Mom. It seemed like every other house in our neighborhood had at least one fruit tree. The most popular were apple and cherry, both of which were growing in the back yard of our second rental house. In later years we enjoyed eating peaches and Concord grapes from the backyard of our house on Park Avenue. I can still remember Mom on a hot summer day in the kitchen with the stove burners going full blast making grape jelly. Mom's hands were always stained purple in the process. Those jars of grape jelly were stored in our basement fruit cellar along with other home canned fruits and vegetables for meals during those long, cold winter months.

Dad carried his lunch to work to help with the food budget as was often done during the Depression; Mary Ellen and I walked home from school for our lunch. In those days, all of the meals were prepared from scratch. There were no heat and eat frozen foods. The kitchen was barely ten feet square, just large enough to hold our Westinghouse electric stove and refrigerator and three feet of counter space on each side of the sink. Our refrigerator had a small freezer compartment designed to hold a couple of ice cube trays and just enough room for a quart container of store bought ice cream which was a rare treat. Usually Mom made her own ice cream which bore little resemblance to the real thing. Our typical dessert was a concoction of Jell-O and canned fruit topped with whipped cream. Since there were no frozen foods then, Mom made frequent trips to the grocery store to purchase everything fresh.

Of course Mary Ellen and I always had to eat all of our vegetables. Mom first said, "eat your vegetables, don't forget the starving Armenians." Her comment didn't mean much to me at the time since I didn't know anyone by that name that lived in the neighborhood. (It wasn't until many years later that I found out the term "Starving Armenians" referred to what happened to Armenia in the early nineteen hundreds when they were invaded by neighboring Turkey. As a result of the Turkish invasion, several hundred thousand Armenians lost their lives from disease, starvation and death marches.) If all else failed, Mom said "eat all of your vegetables or no dessert." That comment worked.

It was a rare treat to eat out in those pre-fast food days. Once in a great while our family enjoyed the selections at Scotten's Cafeteria, a two-block walk from our house. To the best of my knowledge our family never ate a meal at a conventional restaurant during all of those growing up years. My parents never considered dining at one of the few drive-in restaurants scattered around the north side. Our typical away-from-home meals consisted of Sunday afternoon picnics in a park during the summer months or dining with family friends at their home.

During the depression an early recollection was eagerly awaiting Dad's return from the office every evening. Often he brought home a large manila envelope of canceled U.S. postage stamps from his office mail. My sister Mary Ellen and I dumped the stamps in a pile on the living room rug. We sorted out the keepers, soaked the stamps off the paper in a pan of water, dried the stamps on old newspapers, and pasted them into our inexpensive stamp albums. It wasn't long before we started collecting foreign stamps as well. This required sending away to one of the many stamp companies specializing in such material. Two of my favorite stamp sources were the Jamestown Stamp and Coin Company and the Garcelon Stamp Company. I was fascinated with those foreign stamps received on approval every week or two for my buying pleasure. The stamps had been carefully hinged onto individual approval sheets containing twenty five stamps in five rows of five stamps, each with its own purchase price. Many of the foreign stamps were strange shapes such as diamonds and triangles. The foreign stamps were often from exotic sounding countries such as Tannu

Tova and Bosnia and Herzegovina. After a great deal of thought, we removed some of the stamps from the approval sheets to be added to our collections, and the remaining stamps and payment owed were returned within the ten-day deadline. An unexpected benefit of this hobby was the addition to our knowledge of world history and geography. No doubt due to that early start, I have seriously collected postage stamps off and on as an adult. Besides postage stamps, as a kid I collected matchbook covers, coins, postcards, marbles, comic books, airplane models, and political campaign buttons. That early interest in collecting probably influenced my entry into the antiques and collectibles business many years later.

Our hobby of pasting magazine and newspaper articles and photos in our scrapbooks was not unlike pasting postage stamps in an album. The "must keep" scrapbook items ranged from newspaper pictures of popular movie stars to favorite Sunday comic strips. My sister and I also collected movie star photographs that we sent away for to Hollywood. Eagerly awaiting the mailman's delivery every day was part of the fun. After all, for many of us it was about the only personal mail we ever received. When the movie star photo card finally arrived, it was often autographed by the star. Just think, famous movie stars must have taken the time out of their busy schedules to sign the photos, and if I was very lucky I might even receive a personal note as well. My collection of movie star photos ranged from teen-age idol Jane Withers to comics Laurel and Hardy.

Even more popular than most movie stars in the 1930s were the famous Dionne quintuplets. Their claim to fame was being the first and only set of identical quintuplets to have survived into adolescence. There were quintuplet multiple births recorded as early as 999 AD but no other identical set of quintuplets has ever survived to the present time. A set of quintuplets was born to a Hoosier family as early as 1875 with the longest living baby surviving just twenty-one days. The Dionne girls were born on May 28, 1934 to a rural farm family in Ontario, Canada. Their parents already had six other children at the time of their birth and were ill prepared for all of the publicity that was soon thrust on them. The presiding doctor, Allan Roy Dafoe, soon took over the care and feeding of the famous quintuplets and ultimately became their joint guardian by decree of the Ontario government.

Doctor Dafoe exploited their uniqueness in newspaper and magazine articles and on many grocery products. For example, the *Indianapolis Times* devoted space for several years to a series of articles on the life of the quintuplets each time they celebrated a birthday. Of course Dr. Dafoe always authored the articles for the appropriate fee. As the articles appeared in the local newspaper, we carefully cut out the quintuplet's pictures and pasted them in our scrapbooks. Their likenesses also appeared on dolls, mirrors, calendars, cereal bowls, sheet music, books, pillowcases and post cards. The products they sponsored ranged from Link gasoline to Karo syrup. Our Sunday morning pancakes had to be served with Karo syrup, as we didn't want to disappoint Annette Lillianna Marie, Yvonne Edouilda Marie, Cecile Marie Emilda, Marie Rein Alma, and Emilie Marie Jeanne Dionne.

Speaking of doctors, a memorable and frequent occurrence in the early 1930s was catching at least one of the "big four" childhood illnesses: whooping cough, mumps, chicken pox, and measles (choices included three-day, seven-day and German). In those days there were no disease inoculations except for small pox and diphtheria. Being infected by any of the big four diseases was considered a rite of passage from infancy into older childhood. Fortunately, not many children suffered lingering effects. Our parents didn't become infected when we were sick since they were immunized by having had the same diseases many years earlier. Thank goodness for the radio, as it relieved our long days of boredom and discomfort.

As soon as we were sent home by the school nurse Mom called the family doctor to report the health problem. That day or by the next evening at the latest, the doctor visited us at home during his round of house calls. Yes, in those days doctors saw patients at home. After the doctor had confirmed that it was an infectious disease such as whooping cough, and prescribed a remedy, he contacted the local Board of Health. The next day one of their employees showed up and nailed a large cardboard sign on the front of our house saying: "WHOOPING COUGH. THIS PLACARD MUST NOT BE REMOVED EXCEPT BY ORDER OF THE HEALTH SERVICE." It was generally understood that no one was to enter or leave the house during the quarantine period, except for family members.

Little did I realize that one day I would suffer from another malady, crooked teeth. In my early teens the dentist recommended that I have braces put on to straighten my teeth, which looked like they had been crammed into my mouth helter-skelter. As this was a major outlay of money for my parents, there was a lot of soul searching before the decision was made to go ahead with the braces. I was required to visit the orthodontist every Saturday morning for several weeks as he installed the braces and then gradually tightened the bands to align my teeth. In those days having braces installed was akin to medieval torture. First each tooth had to be encircled with a wide metal band which often dug deep into the tender gums. Then wires were connected to all of the bands and the tooth twisting began as the dentist tightened the bands more each week with what looked like a pair of small pliers.

The dentist warned me that with the braces, I shouldn't eat any candy or other sweets. Any new cavities would be nearly impossible to fill, given the braces. Unfortunately I never met a candy I didn't like, except for Horehound which tasted and sounded yucky. I needed to find something else to satisfy my sweet tooth. That is when I got hooked on Sen-Sen, those tiny licorice bits barely 1/8 inch square. Sen-Sen was developed in the late 1800s by a perfume dealer in Rochester, New York. The taste freshener was on the market for several years as a cosmetic and gradually became known as a breath mint. Sen-Sen satiated my craving for sweets and at the same time eliminated that scourge halitosis, more popularly known as bad breath.

The entire family joined in the fun of playing card and board games during those lean Depression years. My family spent many happy evening hours playing card games such as Double Solitaire, Authors, War, Go-Fish, Crazy 8's, and Old Maid. The family's favorite board games were Chinese Checkers, Parcheesi, Uncle Wiggily, Tripoley and of course Monopoly which Parker Brothers released in 1935. Actually Monopoly was only an updated version of the Landlord Game, which was introduced in 1904. In addition to the card and board games, we spent many hours pouring over jigsaw puzzles spread out on the card table. We traded jigsaw puzzles with our neighbors, occasionally finding to our dismay that one or two pieces were missing. Of course that only became obvious after we had fitted together a couple of hundred pieces. If all else failed, we reverted to a thrill packed evening of playing Pick-up-Sticks or Tiddlywinks.

Religion didn't play an important role in our family's life during my formative years and my parents didn't attend church during that period. Perhaps the reason my parents didn't go to church was that they couldn't agree on whether the family should attend a Catholic or Protestant church. Dad had been raised a strict Catholic while Mom's religious background was hazy at best. Consequently when we were children they didn't go to any church and the subject of religion was never discussed openly at home. However after Dad's retirement they became faithful members of a Protestant church for the rest of their lives.

Under my parents' watchful eye every Sunday morning Mary Ellen and I faithfully walked the six blocks from our Park Avenue home to Sunday school at the Meridian Heights Presbyterian Church at 47th and Central Ave. There we sang the usual children's religious songs, listened to bible stories, memorized bible passages, and used crayons to color in the outlines of famous bible figures.

By the time I was a young teenager I became bored with Sunday school and found an alternative at Silver's drug store. There I used my weekly Sunday school allowance for the pinball machine. Fortunately Mary Ellen kept mum on my misadventure. Unfortunately, it wasn't too many Sundays later when a neighbor chanced to see me playing the pinball machine at Silver's and shortly thereafter I was called on the carpet by Mom and Dad. The end result—back to Sunday school.

Every now and then Dad made the dreaded announcement at Saturday evening dinner that the family would visit friends the next afternoon. Sunday visits were certainly not to my liking since I would miss some of my favorite afternoon and early evening radio programs such as Gene Autry, Jack Benny and Charlie McCarthy.

Mom was particularly anxious for us kids to dress nicely for the occasion. It was her chance to see us wear a Christmas or birthday gift we had received from one of her family members in Chicago. It seemed as if our relatives thought we kids only wanted clothing. My sister enjoyed receiving those presents but all I really wanted was something useful like a Buck Rogers space gun or a Dick Tracy sub-machine gun. The relatives never got the message; I usually received a handkerchief, a pair or two of dark dress socks, or a heavy wool scarf, all of which were seldom worn.

For Sunday afternoon visits Mary Ellen often wore a fancy white dress, anklet socks, and Mary Jane shoes. She braided her hair carefully and kept it in place with a Scotty dog barrette. I on the other hand dressed up only under the threat of great bodily harm. I was usually required to put on a starched white shirt, dress tie, and pressed long pants. I also had to polish my seldom worn Buster Brown shoes. Lastly I needed to comb my hair and dab on some Brylcreem to keep it in place. Mom gave us a full dress inspection to detect any lingering problem areas such as dirty hands or finger nails. If she found a problem it was back to the bathroom for repairs.

As luck would have it, our Sunday visits were usually limited to the home of one of Dad's work buddies from Westinghouse rather than a visit with the family of a school chum. That meant my sister and I would have a boring time, especially when we visited a family with no children such as the Krause's. Mind you, nothing was really wrong with Fritz and Hilda Krause, if you were an adult that is. They were friendly, but perhaps Hilda was a bit too friendly as she always wanted to hug us children upon arrival and then give us a peck on the cheek. Ugh.

Before dinner the elders engaged in some polite conversation in the living room while Mary Ellen and I were given a several-hundred-piece jig saw puzzle to work on. The jig saw puzzle was always a picture of something dopey like a scene of "Two Deer Grazing at a Forest Pool at Eventide." Yuk! At home I preferred jig saw puzzles like "Knights of the Table Round in Mortal Combat" and "A Pirate Ship on the High Seas Flying the Jolly Rogers Flag." Of course we kids never finished the puzzle but it did keep us busy and out of the way before supper. For a before dinner refreshment Hilda offered us glasses of warm Ovaltine, a beverage I dislike to this day.

Since the Krause's were of good German stock, we typically had a meal of bratwurst or knockwurst sausage, German potato salad, sauerkraut and beets, all topped off by rhubarb pie for dessert, none of which were my favorites.

After supper I joined Dad and Fritz in the living room where they pulled out their Old Gold cigarettes and lit up. In that smoke filled room fortunately there wasn't "a cough in a carload," as the Old Gold cigarette radio commercial reassured everyone. I had to endure the men's conversation about boring work topics such as invoice processing, and product code changes and the like. Mary Ellen was smart enough to stay in the kitchen and help the ladies clean up after dinner. She listened to Mom and Hilda discuss supposedly interesting women's stuff like the latest cake recipes and home decorating tips, or a particularly interesting article in the latest issue of *Women's Home Companion* magazine. In the meantime I was sitting on the living room sofa bored to tears where I mastered the fine art of eyeball rolling. I could hardly wait for Dad to give the signal that it was time to head for home which meant early to bed because of school the next day.

Our family had only one fancy dinner each week, served punctually at 1:00 PM on Sunday afternoon. Although evening suppers were fine, they just couldn't compare with Sunday dinner. Perhaps the Sunday dinners were so enjoyable because we often had guests from Dad's office—men on temporary work assignment in Indianapolis from other Westinghouse sales offices.

When Sunday dinner was ready on those special occasions, my sister or I struck a small set of portable chimes and ushered the adults into the dining room. Although the use of chimes to announce dinner might appear an affectation, our chimes were a souvenir from Dad's short-term business venture in the early 1920s. He and a brother had operated a small business, the Featherstone Kitching Company in Chicago, which manufactured those chimes.

I always looked forward to the times we had guests, particularly after dinner when we kids joined the adults in the living room. It wasn't often that we had the opportunity to hear about world events other than at school. As young children, we didn't get much news from the daily paper, as the comic strips were our favorite reading material. Even the Pathé newsreel shorts at the local movie houses were only updated once a week, and the type of news they offered was not of much interest to us boys, except the war scenes. If we were lucky, we kids might even be allowed to offer a comment or two during the adult conversation. Fortunately the old adage "children should be seen and not heard" was not part of our growing-up experience at home.

I was told by Dad that his parents, born in the 1850s, had different thoughts on the subject when he was a youngster in the 1890s.

Although there was some table talk at our regular evening meals about current events, Dad never mentioned politics, religion or other serious topics such as crime and natural disasters. He believed that if the talk became too stressful it might lead to another heart attack. He had a severe one at the age of thirty-nine when I was one year old and he was bed ridden for six months. In the early 1930s there wasn't much else available in the way of medical treatment except bed rest. Upon his recovery, Dad took a vow never to become stressed or excited about anything. Consequently politics and the major disasters that captured the headlines were never discussed.

Some of the tragedies in the 1930s that made headline news included the death of humorist Will Rogers in a plane crash in 1935; the crash of the dirigible Hindenburg at Lakehurst, New Jersey, in 1937 with great loss of life; and the kidnapping and death of the Lindbergh baby in 1932. Five years earlier Lindbergh, the Lone Eagle, had become the first man to fly solo across the Atlantic Ocean in his single-engine airplane, the Spirit of St. Louis.

During the 1930s, Dad joined several fraternal and veteran's organizations including the American Legion and the VFW (Veterans of Foreign Wars) faithfully attending every meeting. For a time Mom was a member of the Legion Auxiliary and my sister and I were members of the American Legion Juniors. Dad also joined the Forty & Eight which was formed by American Legionnaires in 1920 as a charitable fraternal organization. Its name originated during World War I when American servicemen in France were transported to the battle front in boxcars which could hold either forty men or eight horses.

Perhaps the most traumatic of Dad's induction rituals was his initiation into the local chapter of the VFW in 1937 at Northern Beach Park, located several miles north of Indianapolis. The initiation ceremony was quite elaborate and never to be forgotten by those who were present. As part of the ceremonies the initiates were required to dress up in women's clothing and parade around the park in black face. At the time this was supposedly the greatest form of humiliation known to mankind. Dad was so embarrassed about what had taken place that day that it was several years before he told us about it and showed us the photograph of himself in drag.

VFW INITIATION RITUAL–NORTHERN BEACH PARK
DAD SEATED FRONT ROW CENTER

Dad enjoyed researching the family genealogy. As a result of his research findings he was eligible and did join the Sons of the American Revolution (SAR) in 1937 although the SAR never had the prestige of its feminine counterpart, the DAR. In the 1930's Dad also joined the Scientech Club, which still holds monthly meetings to hear talks on topics of interest to the membership. I could never have guessed at the time that I would give a talk to the same club sixty years later.

In his spare time at home Dad was a passionate reader of the classics as he had been in his early youth. His continued interest in the classics in later life was partly due to his poor health which greatly limited his physical activities. His one complaint was that he never had anyone to talk to about his reading. When his work and club pals wanted to talk sports, Dad wanted to talk about the eternal verities. Rather than Joe Louis and Babe Ruth, Dad's heroes were Plato and Plutarch. Although Dad was widely read he was not much for giving advice. Whenever I asked his opinion on a decision I was trying to make, his usual response was "Get yourself a piece of paper and a pencil. Make two columns headed by the words Pro and Con, then write down in the appropriate column all the things you can think of that are for or against the idea. Study your entries carefully and decide for yourself what the answer should be."

Dad was mostly self-educated although he had graduated from high school. He firmly believed that a person could become fully self-educated by reading books, not unlike Abraham Lincoln, one of Dad's heroes. In addition to encouraging us children to read library books, Dad insisted that we become familiar with his four favorite home study reference works: Webster's Dictionary, the World Almanac, a set of Funk & Wagnall's Encyclopedias, and his twenty-four volume set of the Book of Knowledge. The latter reference work was a massive source of information on virtually every conceivable subject. It was offered as a "complete and practical course in self-education without equal in the world of 1938." The twenty-four volume set consisted of some ten thousand pages and almost as many photographs. All of the reference works were kept on a library table in our living room for easy access. He also believed in the fine art of writing and kept a daily diary or journal for several years with entries about his activities and personal observations on what went on in the world around him.

By the time I was five, one of the family's Saturday morning rituals was a trip to the Broad Ripple Library. I am indebted to Dad for making this a long-term habit. As a young man he had read and collected the complete works of many famous authors, ranging from Victor Hugo to Shakespeare. His book collection was housed in a large six by seven foot bookcase in my bedroom. His love for classic literature continued for many years, and by 1945 he had completed all six years of the Great Books courses offered at Butler University. At the end of his studies, he was offered the opportunity to teach the university course which he did for the next two years.

In 1938 the Broad Ripple Library moved to the J.S. Mustard Hall building in the 6200 block of North Guilford Ave. The Hall also housed Masonic Lodge No. 643, of which Jacob Mustard had been a member. Jacob Mustard had provided the funds to construct the Lodge building in 1902. (The Broad Ripple Library branch has moved three times since then.) Once a week Dad drove the family there, first in our 1929 Buick and later in our 1933 Buick. The entire family took books home from the library. Some of my favorites as a youngster were *Black Beauty, Hans Brinker and The Silver Skates* and *Humphrey the Box Turtle.* I still have the reading certificate from Broad Ripple Library, received in 1938 for completing the summer reading program. In addition to the library books, I received several books over the years as birthday and Christmas gifts from my parents.

My favorite book as a youngster was Richard Halliburton's *Complete Book of Marvels.* This 316-page behemoth documented his travels around the world. The book was divided for story telling into two geographic sections: the Occident and the Orient. Bobbs-Merrill Company of Indianapolis published the book in 1938. Unfortunately this was to be Halliburton's last book. In 1939 he attempted to sail a Chinese junk of his own design, the *Sea Dragon,* from Hong Kong to the opening of the San Francisco World's Fair. When he was twenty days out to sea, Halliburton and his Chinese crew disappeared in a typhoon and were never heard from again. My interest in reading the *Book of Marvels* had been piqued when our family heard a lecture by Burton Holmes, a nationally recognized world traveler, at the Murat Theater. His 1941 talk was "Adventures of Richard Halliburton in our United States." By 1958 Holmes had given over eight thousand lectures around the world illustrating his travels.

Another source of information on world events and geography was the monthly *National Geographic* magazine. Dad subscribed to it for many years and read each issue from cover to cover. When the current issue had been read by the entire family (I often just looked at the interesting pictures of the native girls) the magazine joined the stack in the basement fruit cellar. My parents' move to Chicago several years later forced them to dispose of the one hundred and fifty plus issue collection.

I augmented library and personal books in the early years with a healthy dose of *Big Little* books and comic books either purchased at the corner drug stores or obtained in trading deals with other boys in the neighborhood. For some reason *Big Little* books really never caught on in our neighborhood. Perhaps it was because they were very small as their name suggested, about four inches by four inches. Consequently the illustrations in drab black and white didn't have the visual impact of the larger comic book illustrations in color.

By the time I was fourteen years old I had accumulated a six-foot high stack of comic books. Ironically they were stacked in my bedroom next to the large bookcase that held Dad's collection of classic literature. My comic books were obtained from a steady succession of boys knocking on our front door, trading me their comic books for firecrackers that I had stockpiled from previous acquisitions. My comic collection included many of the early classics starting with the first issues of *Superman, Batman, Action*, the *Green Hornet* and *Captain Marvel*. At the end of WW II, I donated all of my comics to the wounded veterans recuperating at the Veterans Hospital on Cold Springs Road in Indianapolis. Reading comic books and more serious literature borrowed from the public library was in the process of being usurped by my favorite radio programs. After all, listening to the radio required very little effort. In fact, I discovered that it could be done with my eyes closed.

Unlike Dad, Mom was not interested in discussing the eternal verities, perhaps because her eighth grade education did not include reading the classics. Mom was a prolific reader but her tastes focused on womens' magazines of the day such as *McCalls, Good Housekeeping, Family Circle*, and *Women's Home Companion*. When we arrived home from school we often found Mom in the living room reading one of her magazines after most of her household chores were finished for the day.

As children, both Mary Ellen and I had a series of chores to do inside and outside the house. We were expected to help Dad keep the property looking neat throughout the year. In summer when we were old enough, we cut the front and back grass. This was not an easy job, since our push mower was a heavy, cast iron monster. We also raked the grass clippings, and in the fall we raked leaves, and shoveled snow in the winter. We helped take down the storm windows and replace them with screens in the spring and did the reverse in the fall. Another chore was helping Mom hang the wash outside when weather allowed. After our evening meal my sister and I cleared off the supper dishes. When we were older we washed, dried and put the dishes away. My experience as a dishwasher later came in handy in college. To earn extra money I washed dishes in our fraternity house. Later I washed mountains of pots and pans, dishes, trays, and tableware while on K.P. (kitchen police) detail in the Army. Another chore was helping Mom clean the rugs. We used a hand operated Bissell sweeper on the rugs (electric vacuum cleaners were virtually unknown) and a long handled dust mop on the hardwood floors.

One of my chores as I got older was taking care of the coal-burning furnace during cold winter months. This daily chore included stoking the furnace with several shovels full of coal from the coal bin. Care was taken that the coal dust in the bin not be disturbed, or it could find its way into the main basement room where the wash usually hung in cold or rainy weather. Next I took a six-foot stoker rod, opened the furnace door carefully, and jabbed the heavy steel rod into the firebox. The idea was to break up any clinkers (large lumps of fused coal) into small pieces and make more air holes in the firebox so the coal burned more efficiently. Finally I shook the firebox louvers slowly so that all the residual ash fell into the ash pit at the base of the furnace. Then weekly, the cooled ashes were shoveled carefully ("Don't get the basement wash dirty!") into paper bags and carried out to the back alley. The city set aside one day a week for ash collection by men walking down the alleys beside mule drawn wagons. The wagons, usually three or four hooked together, had high sides and were open at the top. Heavy wide canvas covers were suspended from the wagon ridgepoles to keep the ash from blowing around when the wagon was in motion.

Another weekday was set aside for garbage collection since most of the refuse was discarded food (no garbage disposals) and not trash. After dinner every evening, either my sister or I carried the food scraps out to a large metal garbage can at the alley. Since we had a deep back yard, the odor of rotting food never reached our house. However, the neighborhood dogs roaming the area usually found and knocked over the cans, scattering the contents far and wide. No dog leash laws then! We frequently had the chore of cleaning up the debris.

There wasn't much trash in those days since many food items came in bulk with little packaging required. Grocery sacks were not used much, because many housewives shopped daily and carried their own cloth net shopping bags to the store while the daily newspapers and magazines were saved for the school paper drive. Since all soft drinks and beer were sold in returnable glass bottles with a two-cent deposit, they rarely found their way into neighborhood trash. On the odd chance that someone had mistakenly discarded returnable bottles with their trash, the bottles never made it to the city dump. Right before trash pickup, we boys roamed the alleys looking for bottles to return to the corner stores for the two cent-a-bottle reward.

Dad had always been a General Motors man, just as some of my friends' fathers were Ford men or Chrysler men. For example, the father of my best friend Dick Rhude, was a Desoto man through and through. During the late 1940's and 1950's he traded in his last year's model for a new one every year. I was quite impressed with this conspicuous form of consumption, since during all those years Dad continued to drive his old 1940 Pontiac. What was even more impressive was that Dick's father had his new Desoto hand washed and waxed every Saturday at the Pure Oil Station located at the corner of College Avenue and 54th Street. When the De Soto sparkled liked new it was parked by an attendant near the corner sidewalk that bordered the service station for all passersby to see. Since Dick's father was an insurance salesman no doubt he hoped to leave the impression with prospective customers that a shiny looking new auto was a sure sign of a successful businessman.

To save money Dad washed and waxed the car himself at home in the early days. When Mary Ellen and I were tall enough to reach the top of the 1933 Buick, we were allowed to wax the car with Simonize to earn a little spending money. That's when I realized just how large our 1933 Buick really was, from the tip of the fancy hood ornament, past the two side wheel mounts to the trunk mounted on the rear luggage carrier which extended beyond the rear bumper. In those days our car like many others had pull-down cloth window shades and a place for a bud vase. What it didn't have were seat belts, power brakes, power steering, an automatic transmission, or turn indicators.

During the cold winter evenings the car was always hooked up to a battery charger in the garage. If all else failed and the engine didn't turn over after a full charge, Dad had to hand crank the car to get it started. I looked forward to the day when I would be old enough to do likewise. Little did I know how many sprained and broken wrists resulted from trying to crank a car by hand. Another winter problem was the lack of heat in the car. Many cars during that period didn't have inside heat, since heaters were sold as optional equipment. If there was a car heater, often it did not generate enough warmth to heat the rear compartment. That was the case with our car's heater. On very cold days, Mary Ellen and I in the back seat needed to cover ourselves with a wool lap robe which hung on the back of the front seat when not in use.

Another winter chore was jacking up the car and switching to winter tires which often had embedded metal studs for better traction. Those tires made quite a racket on the snow cleared pavement. A few years later they were outlawed because of the damage they caused to the street surfaces. Tire chains were also available for use during heavy snows. We didn't use chains because they were a real nuisance to mount on the tires. Chains also made quite a racket on plowed streets. During World War II old tires were often recapped due to the rubber shortage. Unscrupulous tire dealers re-grooved tires that had all of their tread worn off and sold them as recaps.

We finally traded in the 1933 Buick for a stodgy four-door 1940 Pontiac in the late 1940s. I was very disappointed in Dad's choice. I hoped that he would buy a Nash Ambassador with its advanced styling and seats that converted into a double bed. Now that was keen. I could just imagine our family pulling into a service station and asking the attendant to change the oil and oh yes, change the sheets as well.

As we approached our teenage years my relationship to Mary Ellen was what I liken to a shaky truce between two warring nations. Mary Ellen was always accusing me of something such as going into her bedroom, finding the key to her private diary, opening the lock and reading her most intimate thoughts. Of course she was wrong. I didn't need her key as I could open her diary lock with either a paper clip or a hairpin.

One of my earliest skirmishes with my sister was over the Sunday comics. I finally figured out that the only way to win was to get up early enough to grab the paper as soon as the newsboy delivered it. The plan worked, and at 6:00 AM I was the first one to read the comic strips. My favorites were *Popeye*, the *Katzenjamer Kids* and *Bringing up Father*.

Mary Ellen and I read our share of popular children's books during that period. I preferred the *Hardy Boys* and *Dave Dawson of the Dawn Patrol* series. However, for a change of pace I sometimes sneaked into Mary Ellen's bedroom and borrowed one of her Nancy Drew mystery stories. I read it quickly and put it back in her bookcase before she was the wiser.

Another favorite sibling foray was what I called sneak and peek. Often Mary Ellen had one of her school chums over after school. As soon as they entered the house, they locked themselves in her bedroom. Being a very inquisitive kid, I wanted to know what they were doing in there. I surreptitiously climbed out of a second floor window in my parents' bedroom, which led to the roof of the front porch. I crept over to my sister's bedroom window and cautiously peeked in to see what the two of them were up to. Much to my disappointment, they were usually doing homework or something equally humdrum.

By our teen-age years, my sister and I finally joined forces. Our personal privacy had become an important issue. We decided that we needed to find a secret language that we could use without fear of being understood by our parents, teachers, or any other adult. We decided against Pig Latin because we thought that most adults probably knew how to decode it. We considered Esperanto, the international language that we had heard about at school. That language had been around since 1878, when the first book was written in Esperanto. The language really never caught on but almost became a reality in the 1920s when the League of Nations held a vote to make it their working language. At the time, French was recognized as the international language. It is not hard to guess which country cast the one deciding dissenting vote. In the 1930s both Adolph Hitler writing *Mien Kampf* and Stalin in speeches characterized Esperanto as unpatriotic and the work of international spies and troublemakers. But Mary Ellen and

I vetoed the idea simply because the language was too difficult to learn.

Asking around, we found a language that served the purpose—it was simple to learn and seemed hard to decipher. It was called the Op language. (Op rhymes with cop). To speak the language, it was relatively easy to insert the syllable Op before every vowel in a word. However, to do so properly the speaker had to be a good speller and have a good understanding of word syllables. For example, the word "taken" was pronounced as top-a-cop-en and "become" was pronounced as bop-e cop-o-mop-e. It worked! Our parents didn't have a clue. Mary Ellen and her chums used it frequently particularly on the telephone party line. My problem was that most of my friends didn't know the Op language and didn't want to learn it. Thus in time I had to depend on just speaking English. My two years of studying Spanish in high school were not of much value either. I could only say, "Donde esta Usted?" (Where are you?) and "Vaya con Dios!" (Go With God). Unfortunately those two Spanish expressions didn't come in very handy in day to day conversation with my classmates.

Our family, like most families during the 1930s and 1940s, stayed close to home. We never ventured out of the state, except for short visits to relatives in Chicago or a brief summer stay in Wisconsin. Therefore I was quite envious of Mary Ellen when she announced at dinner one evening in 1946 that she had an opportunity to work that summer at the Kimball House resort in Bar Harbor, Maine with one of her high school friends, Pat Capehart. Pat's father, Senator Capehart, managed to get them jobs as waitresses at the Kimble House Lodge and Restaurant the coming summer. While she worked in Bar Harbor that summer it seemed strange to have the table set for three at dinner after all those meals with the four of us.

Upon her return from Bar Harbor right before her senior year in high school began in the fall, she announced that she had a surprise for us by the name of Hester. I wondered if it was going to be a dog or possibly a cat. Mary Ellen took us outside and said," I would like you to meet my very best friend Hester." Her friend was a very used 1937 four-door Buick convertible with side mounted tires, which my sister had purchased in Bar Harbor for one hundred and fifty dollars. The car looked as if it were on its last legs or wheels as the case may be.

The paint job, a rusty maroon, looked as if it had been applied with a broom. Since the car was purchased topless, my sister had the Kimball House laundry sew a top for it out of white canvas.

MARY ELLEN AND HESTER ON PARK AVENUE

To help recoup her initial investment, Mary Ellen charged her fellow Kimball House employees fifty cents each to autograph the white top and another fifty cents to ride around Bar Harbor in that Buick behemoth. According to her own recollection, on her trip home she carried sixty quarts of drain oil stored in the trunk and back seat of her car. The used motor oil had been donated by various Bar Harbor service stations before the trip home. Since the car burned one quart of oil every twenty five miles, she figured that the used motor oil didn't stay in the engine long enough to do any real damage. Her Buick was one of the few cars whose miles per gallon were about the same for motor oil as for gasoline. At highway speeds Hester discharged such a thick cloud of blue smoke that the plume can still be seen today hovering over that route back home. That car did indeed make a statement when parked in front of our house on Park Avenue much to my parent's embarrassment. A few months later the car mysteriously disappeared never to be seen again.

Mary Ellen and her friend Pat so enjoyed being on their own the summer of 1946 that they spent the next two summers working as waitresses at Camp Curry, Yosemite National Park in California.

Soon after the arrival of Hester, Mary Ellen announced that she had another surprise for the family that would mystify and delight our taste buds. It became known as the infamous kitchen caper. She said that she had purchased a special edible which she had learned about from one of her more avant-garde Shortridge High School chums, Lucy Littell. That next day Mom rather reluctantly let my sister do her thing in the kitchen right before supper time. Dad and I were indeed mystified since whatever Mary Ellen was cooking had a strange odor reminiscent of Mom's boiling cabbage.

As soon as dinner was served, Mary Ellen excused herself to retrieve the mystery item. She returned from the kitchen with great pomp and circumstance carrying a small platter and announced triumphantly, "These are artichokes!" The rest of us took one look and gasped with horror. The things looked like a cross between a hand grenade and a small, green pine cone. I thought, what is an artichoke and why would you want to try and eat it? My sister advised us that artichokes were served as an appetizer before dinner in the best of families. Not to be deterred, she then demonstrated the proper technique for eating this strange looking thing.

She proceeded to tear off a leaf, dip it into a sauce and pop the concoction into her mouth. She slowly removed the meat from the leaf while clamping it tightly with her teeth. I thought, how disgusting. First you put the thing in your mouth and then you take it right back out. Throwing caution to the wind, the rest of us reluctantly joined in this strange eating ritual until the artichokes were just a pile of ragged leaves. Did the family enjoy eating the artichokes? As I remember, we didn't have artichokes with supper again for a long—long time.

Not long after, Mary Ellen announced that she had prepared another dining delight for the family. The first thing I noticed when seated at the table was a long and thin paper wrapper placed next to each of our dinner plates with strange markings that looked like hieroglyphics. Then my sister appeared from the kitchen carrying a covered tureen and wearing an unusual looking costume. I knew that it wasn't Halloween so there must have been some other reason for the costume. Mary Ellen then bowed and announced that we were going to eat a real Chinese dinner hence her Oriental outfit. This came as a shock to me. At home we had never eaten a truly foreign dish, just good old reliable American food which Mom cooked with great expertise.

MARY ELLEN GONE ASIATIC

Uncovering the tureen my sister said dramatically, "this is Chow Mein!" Chow Mein I thought, what is Chow Mein? The only Chow I knew was a dog owned by the landlady in the Chicago apartment building where my grandmother lived. That Chow was large, mean and scary. I wondered if we were going to eat dog meat. However, my sister reassured us that the dark lumps of meat in the mix were really beef. She explained that Chow Mein was considered a Chinese delicacy and that Chow Mein actually meant fried noodles in Chinese.

Next my sister instructed us to rip open the paper wrapper which contained two wooden sticks. She said that they were called chop sticks and showed us how to use them. We watched as she picked up the chop sticks, and deftly gathered up a sizeable amount of Chow Mein which she then popped in her mouth. The rest of us tried to follow suit with varying degrees of success.

That meal seemed to take forever. I thought it no wonder that the Chinese were so thin; they never had enough time to eat a large meal if they had to use Chop sticks. We all agreed that my sister's Chow Mein was tasty but was it really worth all that effort? Of course she made sure that each of us had dessert in the form of a Chinese fortune cookie as a reward for eating the Chow Mein. I still don't know how they insert that small strip of paper with the printed fortune into that tiny opening in the baked cookie.

As to Mary Ellen's Oriental costume, I didn't have the presence of mind to ask where she got it. Although our family never had another formal Chinese dinner, my sister did wear that costume from time to time on special occasions. As far as Chinese food in general was concerned, in the ensuing years our family did get hooked on my Mom's chop suey. I seriously doubt that her chop suey ever resembled the real thing but we sure loved it and oh, by the way, no chopsticks were required.

Soon after the kitchen capers were over Mary Ellen announced one evening at the dinner table that she had gained the powers to predict the future with great accuracy. The rest of the family looked at her as if she was a couple of cards short of a full deck. Not to be intimidated, she said that we could also gain the same mystical power under her tutelage. So that night rather than play the usual family game of Chinese checkers or Tripoley, we reluctantly agreed to be her captive audience. As we sat down around the card table, Mary Ellen reached under her chair and produced two strange looking wooden objects. She said dramatically, this is an Ouija Board and this is a planchette. She went on to explain that the Ouija Board could answer questions about the future by moving the small three cornered wooden planchette slowly around the Ouija board. The alphabet letters, numbers 1-10 and the words Yes and No were printed around the edges of the board. She demonstrated how to use this mystery device by asking it a simple question and then proceeding to move the planchette slowly around the board with two fingers of each hand until it stopped on the word Yes. Her question had been: Do I have mystical powers? The rest of use took turns with the Ouija board under her watchful eye with varying degrees of success. She went on to explain that two individuals could move the planchette together for even more startling results. We tried this approach but were never able to make any sense out of the joint effort. None of the words we spelled by moving the planchette around the board in tandem were recognizable. The Ouija board quickly became ancient history.

It turns out that the Ouija board has been around since before the turn of the 20th century and only came into prominence when it was manufactured by William Fuld starting in 1901. His family continued to manufacture the item until 1966 when Parker Brothers purchased the rights to it. Many variations of the original Ouija board known as Talking Boards are still being sold today.

The one fun game Dad and I played in our backyard was horseshoes. In the 1930s and 1940s it was a very popular outdoor sport. Every park had its horseshoe pits and they were usually occupied by team play. It was the one game Dad played, since he believed it was not too strenuous for his heart condition. The equipment consisted of four iron horseshoes and two iron stakes placed in the ground forty feet apart. Each contestant, taking turns, used two horseshoes to try and ring the distant iron stake. If there were no ringers (they were valued at three points), any horseshoes which landed within six inches of the stake were awarded one point. In our early years I was given a handicap, allowing me to move up several feet toward the opposing stake when throwing the horseshoes. I looked forward to the day when Dad considered me old enough to be thought of as a grownup. That's the day when he would make me throw the horseshoes from behind the same line that he used.

The other member of our family was Skippy, our Cocker Spaniel. Several of my friends had dogs as pets, and I thought that a large dog such as a German shepherd would be great. However my parents told me that our small house and yard were more suitable for a small dog. Thus, we compromised on Skippy. He and I became close friends, so close that when Skippy had a bad case of fleas, so did I. Skippy was let out to roam the neighborhood every morning and returned in the late afternoon for his supper. He was let out again in the early evening for his nighttime prowls and howls. No thought was given to his safety or freedom, since street traffic was light and there were no leash laws. One day some twelve years after he joined the family, Mom let Skippy out in the early evening as usual to roam the neighborhood. When he didn't return a while later we searched the neighborhood over the next several days but never found him. We were upset and saddened at his disappearance as it was like losing a member of the family.

Times were not always idyllic in my home as far as I was concerned. Mom decided we children should learn to play the piano and dance as well. The one extravagance in our home was a used spinet piano that Dad purchased for Mom soon after they were married. Mom had learned to play the piano as a youngster and played quite well by ear. It was her one pleasure in life to forget the dull, tiring household chores that consumed most of her time. Believing that my sister and I should learn to play the piano as well, she hired Mrs. Long, a piano teacher who lived in the neighborhood and made house calls. Mrs. Long stopped by our house once a week to teach us a new tune or two and see how we were progressing. Her arrival in the afternoon after school was not to my liking, nor was the time that Mom set aside for our daily practice. Piano practice was in direct conflict with my important afternoon radio shows. I also seemed to lack the coordination that is required to become a pianist. My right and left hands seemed to be strangers at the keyboard, each hand wanting to go its own separate way. It wasn't long before I put away the sheet music for good. However, as a result of taking the lessons, I did learn to play a rather good rendition of Chopsticks and Tweedle Dum and Tweedle Dee. Since the piano lessons were expensive, they were a luxury our family could ill afford unless we were making real progress. Mary Ellen persevered at piano lessons for a couple of more years, but finally put away her sheet music as well.

As far as formal dance lessons were concerned, I had no interest during those seventh and eighth grade years because I thought that girls were dumb (I was really too timid to go to dance school). Also, I did not want to suffer through the mandatory dance reviews that were held for parents and the few other interested adults. The two north side dance studios were the George W. Lipps School of Dance on North College Avenue and the Mrs. William Byram Gates Dancing Studio on north Delaware Street, housed in the Propylaeum. It would be several more years before I learned to trip the light fantastic, trip being the operative word.

In the early 1940s as a pre-teenager, I became infatuated with the drum as a musical instrument. I had heard big band radio broadcasts and seen Gene Krupa starring with the Tommy Dorsey Orchestra in a live performance at the Circle Theater. Perhaps his most famous drum solo was during the instrumental piece "Drum Boogie" which allowed him to show off his many talents with the sticks. About the same time a neighborhood buddy, Dave Winger, also played the drums which he kept in his bedroom. When we went to Dave's house for a little touch football, he first gave us guys a brief drum solo which impressed me no end. As a result of this conditioning I was ready to buy a drum at the first opportunity. I thought that it should be a lot easier to play than the piano. My chance came as a freshman at Shortridge High. One of the girls in my homeroom, Ann Fuller, mentioned that her brother wanted to sell some drum equipment. It didn't hurt matters that she was one of the cutest girls in school and also a cheerleader. I bashfully let her know that I was interested. I had saved up some cash for just such a venture and my parents gave me a very reluctant okay. I contacted Ann's older brother and soon was the proud owner of a drum set which consisted of a snare drum, a foot operated cymbal and a pair of wood drum sticks and wire brushes.

I set up the drum ensemble in my upstairs bedroom and tried to accompany various pieces of big band music as I listened on my portable radio. I had purchased the drum in the very depth of the summer when the heat and humidity were at their zenith. Our house was typically closed up during the daytime and the heat was trapped on the second floor. In the early evening when I wanted to play the drum, I opened both of my bedroom windows as wide as possible for some cross ventilation. The problem was that our next door neighbor's house was only a few feet away and one of my bedroom windows was directly across from theirs. Our neighbors had always been very friendly but from then on they weren't so friendly. They never came right out and said anything but if looks could kill, I would have been pushing up daises. In addition, my parents were very unhappy about the noise emanating from my bedroom. Fortunately for the neighbors and my family, I didn't stay with the drums very long and sold the set to another unsuspecting would-be musician.

Still believing that I had some talent for music, I purchased a harmonica from Danner Brothers 5 cents to $1.00 Store in Broad Ripple, in hopes that I would find my niche in the world of music. I thought of the harmonica as a perfect solution to my problem, since it was inexpensive and lightweight, and learning to play it did not require formal lessons. I thought of it as a perfect pocket piano. I had been introduced to the harmonica through the antics of Borrah Minevitch and the Rascals during movie shorts at the Uptown Theater. Borrah had formed a group of young harmonica players in the 1920s and had a popular following well into the 1950s. During that period the group performed in over two dozen movie shorts and appeared in several feature movies. They seemed to be having a lot of fun, particularly Johnny Puleo, a midget, who was featured in their act. Johnny played a huge bass harmonica while the tallest member of the music group played a tiny three-inch-long soprano harmonica.

The Indiana humorist Herb Shriner was also noted for his harmonica playing in the 1930s and 1940s. From time to time I heard him on network radio programs, and by 1948 he had his own program on CBS radio, *Herb Shriner Time*. A year later he had his own television show on CBS, the *Herb Shriner Show*. Herb was actually born in Toledo, Ohio but as he said, "I moved to Indiana as soon as I heard about it." Early on he had a harmonica quartet and later marketed his very own *Hoosier Boy* harmonica. My love/hate relationship with the harmonica was followed in quick succession by a Jew's harp and a sweet potato, also known as an ocarina. I finally settled on a kazoo, which took the least amount of talent and unfortunately produced the least soothing music. As a result I was relegated to my bedroom with the door shut and the windows closed if I wanted to play it in the house. Actually I was ahead of my time, since Indiana humorist Gene Shepherd, noted for the movie *The Christmas Story*, became quite proficient on the kazoo and featured it in many of his early radio broadcasts. My venture into the world of music was not to be. I just didn't have the talent. I discovered that it was a lot easier to play the radio.

Perhaps no other invention had as dramatic an impact on my growing up as the radio. As a young child it was my primary source of news, entertainment, and to some extent, education. As with most middle class families during the early Depression years, we had only one radio. It was a large wooden 1930s radio/record player console model Westinghouse that sat high on wooden legs. In those days the radio was recognized as a legitimate piece of furniture, and therefore it was prominently displayed in our living room. I doubt that we would have had such a grand model if Dad had not worked for Westinghouse at the time and received an employee discount on all company products.

Who can forget those wonderful old-time action radio serials such as *Superman, The Shadow, The Green Hornet, The Lone Ranger, Buck Rogers of the 25th Century* and Marshal Matt Dillon of *Gunsmoke* fame. Whether we boys and girls knew it or not we were all intimately involved with the production of those programs. In our mind's eye as we listened to a favorite radio serial we became the set designer, prop man, hair stylist, costume designer, makeup man, set location specialist and casting director, aided by the efforts of the sound effects man. Probably our first real exposure to the theater of the mind was a popular children's radio program of the late 1930s to mid-1950s, *Let's Pretend.* Who can forget the opening salutation from Uncle Bill, "Hel-loooooo Pretenders" followed by a commercial jingle that began, "Cream of Wheat is so good to eat; yes we have it every day."

If asked we could describe our favorite radio programs in detail from what the setting looked like, where the action took place, to a detailed description of the hero. For example, when we listened to the western *Gunsmoke*, we were sure that the radio hero Marshal Dillon was a tall, young, handsome, muscular, lean, two fisted, straight talking and straight shooting law man. Little did we know at the time that the radio part of Marshal Dillon was played by William Conrad who was a short, dumpy, balding, older man who sported a large mustache. He admittedly did have the right voice for the role of Marshal. Of course when radio action serials and soap operas were replaced by television programming, all the fun of using our imaginations went away as well.

As with most single-radio families, the radio was controlled by my parents. Fortunately on the weekend nights and when our homework was done during the school week, our family could agree on what to listen to. We all liked the comedians such as Jack Benny, Bob Hope, and Fred Allen. In addition we tuned in to the weekly situation comedies including *Fibber McGee and Molly*, *The Great Gildersleeve*, *Blondie,* and *Duffy's Tavern–"Where the elite meet to eat."*

When the radio wasn't on Dad listened to one of his favorite classical composers such as Bach, Beethoven or Brahms on the radio console record player. The recordings he treasured were promoted as the World's Greatest Music in brightly colored albums of orange and turquoise. Each album had a four-page history of the life of the recorded composer and some comments on that particular piece of music. Dad's collection of 78-RPM classical albums was carefully stored in the dining room buffet. He purchased the record albums during our weekly trips to the 38th Street A & P Market.

When no one else was around as a teenager I played my favorite records, recorded by Spike Jones and his City Slickers, two of which were *Pass the Biscuits, Mirandy* and *Der Feuhrer's Face*. Mary Ellen preferred the mellow music of Carmen Caballero and his piano. Our family purchased not only classical records at the A & P but our "fine" china as well, through those wonderful in-store promotions. The service station china give-a-ways later supplemented the A & P china.

My sister and I had the choice of listening to what my parents wanted to hear on the radio or finding something else to do. However, all that changed the Christmas when Mary Ellen was ten and I was eight. We each received our very own Westinghouse bedside radio as a present from Santa. Now we could decide what we listened to. For me it was a daily dose of the late afternoon radio serials and the *Lone Ranger* and his faithful Indian companion Tonto after supper. I also liked the capers of Jack, Doc and Reggie in *I Love a Mystery* with that scary theme music.

The radio was particularly valuable during those long days when I was at home from school sick. Basically all that was offered during the morning and early afternoon were the popular soap operas. Appropriately named, these daily serial dramas were usually sponsored by manufacturers of soap products such as Duz, Rinso and Oxydol. Who can forget those radio soap flake commercials? "*Duz* does everything best." "*Rinso* White, Rinso bright. Happy little washday song." "*Oxydol*, The soap that does everything best in your washing machine." "*Ivory* soap is 99.9% pure and it floats." "No dish pan hands with *Lux* soap." "*Dreft*, Gentle as a Mother's touch." "*Vel*—It's MarVELous!" and "*Joy*—From grease to shine in half the time."

Being a somewhat sickly child, I got to know all of the soap opera characters and story lines as well as the soap jingles. This interest in the radio soaps carried over to the summer months when I often listened to the radio in the early morning before getting involved in the usual kid activities of the day. The characters on the programs seemed to lead much more interesting lives than I did. I knew that everything was for the best for Chichi and Papa David in his "Slightly Read Bookshop" on *Life Can be Beautiful*. I knew that everything would one day work out for *Mary Noble*, a stenographer from Iowa who married a matinee idol, "the dream sweetheart of a million other women." Perhaps my favorite was *Stella Dallas*, a poor seamstress whose beloved daughter Lolly Baby married into wealth and society. "Would Stella have to sever her relationship with her daughter Laurel Grosvenor due to their differences in taste and worlds? Stay tuned!" My problem was that I wanted to stay tuned even after school started in the fall. On more than one occasion I feigned illness so that I could stay home and listen to those soaps. For some reason I can't abide the TV soaps today.

By the time I was ten years old I was also hooked on the fifteen-minute radio serials which aired every weekday afternoon from four to six. Those back to back programs included *Jack Armstrong, The All American Boy, Terry and the Pirates*, (the sound of cymbals and gongs and then *Terrrr—eeeeee and the Pirates), Hop Harrigan, CX-4 calling control tower* and *Sgt. Preston in the Challenge of the Yukon!* As a result of listening to *Jack Armstrong*, all of us boys ate Wheaties, the Breakfast of Champions. Of course we had to send in the necessary box tops and a few coins to receive the latest radio premium. I mailed in for several premiums including Jack Armstrong's secret bombsight and his pedometer which, when fastened to the belt, could tell me how far I walked every day.

One of my favorite radio programs was the *Quiz Kids*, starring that mathematical whiz Joel Kupperman. All of the boys and girls on the program had IQ's over 160, and Joel was no exception with an IQ over two hundred. Oddly enough he didn't begin to walk or talk until he was eighteen months old. In a 1944 program when Joel was six years old, he was asked how many seconds there were in a year. After about a half-minute pause, Joel said in a childish drawl "31,536,000 seconds." After a few more seconds elapsed Joel said, "it should be 31,622,400 seconds since this is Leap Year."

Another of my favorite radio programs, which was adapted from a comic strip in the early 1930s, was *Buck Rogers in the 25th Century*. Of course Buck had to have a beautiful sidekick, Wilma Deering, the friendship of a brilliant scientist, Dr. Huer, and an evil adversary, Killer Kane. The story line focused on action in outer space and the solar system with the fate of the universe usually hanging in the balance. Buck guided a robot rocket ship around the galaxy using a radio vision transmitter. What was perhaps the most fascinating part of the adventure series were the great scientific inventions of the day. Who can forget the gyrocosmic relativator, the psychic restrictor ray, the atomic disintegrator, and the ultrasonic death ray? We could certainly use some of those weapons in our country's military arsenal today.

A popular hobby for young teenage boys was searching out "foreign" radio stations late at night when the signals were strongest. We kept a detailed log of the radio stations found throughout the country including their call letters and city of origin. The idea was to see who could find the most faraway stations. As a guide we purchased a radio log book published by RCA listing all of the nation's larger radio stations. At the time, radio stations ranged in power from a high of 50,000 watts such as Cincinnati's station WLW down to a low of 100 watts such as Anderson's station WHBU. Three of the advantages of the radio over the local movie theater were that radio listening was free, close at hand and we could listen while doing something else.

By the time we were teenagers it was music, music, music heard on big band broadcasts and *The Hit Parade* that featured the top ten most popular recording hits of the week. When we were of driving age, we tuned our car radios to station KLAC from Gallatin, Tennessee as we circled the local drive-in restaurants. It was time for *Randy's Record Roundup* of rhythm and blues, sponsored by Royal Crown Pomade, a hair dressing known as the "Silky Straight Hair Pomade." All of the records heard on the program were rhythm and blues played by featured black artists.

Neighborhood Doings

AROUND THE BLOCK

We were fortunate to live in a neighborhood where the house lots were quite narrow, often only thirty to forty feet wide. As a result, on our block there were lots of houses with lots of children. Usually the houses were so close together that when a neighbor sneezed inside his house, even with the windows closed, someone in an adjoining house said "God Bless You." The smaller bungalows were often starter homes for young married couples. Since our block had sidewalks, mothers didn't have to worry about our safety when we were outdoors. They could stay inside and continue with their household chores. We pre-school kids were free to "roam" our block looking for playmates, without having to cross busy streets. In the summer months Mary Ellen and I spent almost all of our waking hours playing outside with boys and girls who lived on our block.

THE CARROLLTON GANG
First Row: Richard Coleman, Raymond Featherstone, Mary Ellen Featherstone
Second Row: Richard Jackson, Mary Jane Coleman, Lacarda Johnson

The following will describe what constituted a neighborhood when children were too young to ride street bicycles. The length of our neighborhood was limited to the houses that lined both sides of the long block we lived on, twenty-five houses in all. The width of our neighborhood was the distance between the two alleys behind the houses on both sides of our street. Consequently, alleys were always shared with the adjoining neighborhoods that consisted of houses facing on the next streets over. As pre-teens we were not wise to venture off the block we lived on without knowing the territory. Did the next neighborhood have a resident bully? Were older boys hanging around looking for trouble? Each neighborhood had its own set of kids' values and rules.

The alley behind our house was used as an auto thoroughfare early in the morning and late in the afternoon, as cars left and entered rear property garages. The alley was also used weekly by the city for ash and trash collection. To us boys trash day was treasure day. It was amazing the things we could find and take home that other people had thrown away. The third and most important role of the alley was as a playground for kids. Most of the alleys were paved and typically about fourteen feet wide.

Not only the streets but the alleys also were swept clean by the massive street sweepers we loved to follow on our bicycles. Our alley had an additional attraction, a small hill that was not found on either adjoining street. The hill was great for roller skating and coasting down on our bicycles or wagons. Unlike the city streets, cars were seldom seen in the alleys during the day. Feeling that the alley was safe, our parents allowed us to use it freely.

It was fun for us boys to walk down the alley and look into the neighbors' back yards. From the street very little could be seen of the deep, narrow backyards, since the houses were so close together that our view was blocked. From the alley, we could answer such important questions as did the house have a rear swing set that we could use? Did they have a dog penned up that we could pet if it was friendly? Did they have a back yard fishpond that would be fun to mess around with? Fortunately there were not many fences separating houses at the side and rear of the properties. The few existing fences were low chain-link fences, easy to see through and climb over. It was another matter if we wanted to walk down an unknown alley as a shortcut to a friend's house in the next neighborhood. Any given alley could be a war zone or neutral territory. We needed to know the lay of the land before daring to venture down a foreign alley.

The same held true for adjoining streets, as they might be no-kids lands. Generally the safest streets for the young kids in our neighborhood to use without fear of possible trouble were the major east-west streets such as 54th Street, leading to the corner retail shops along College Avenue. Since there was a constant stream of adults walking to and from the stores, safe passage was assured. The adults were the unsuspecting peacekeepers of their day. Once we boys and girls were old enough to ride street bikes, the definition of what constituted our neighborhood broadened greatly.

Like other local neighborhoods, the houses along Park Avenue had front sidewalks which could be used for activities like roller skating, hopscotch, jump rope and jacks (girls only!), and tricycle riding for the younger children. To the envy of the rest of us, one kid rode an "Irish Mail." It was like no other speedster I had ever seen. The vehicle used the mechanical principle of an early railroad handcar, which required the movement of a hand lever to propel the car. The name Irish Mail came from the handcar's use as a mail carrier in the old west between railroad camps often populated by Irish immigrants.

On warm summer nights we youngsters caught fireflies and put them in glass jars with metal screw caps which had been punched to make small air holes. We also put in a bed of grass for the fireflies to sleep on. We also enjoyed watching the bats at twilight. They swept down the street seemingly from nowhere, looking for an insect dinner. Another fun evening activity for the young children was the candle-light parade. We boys and girls found empty cardboard shoeboxes and cut several square holes in their sides. We then pasted small pieces of the Sunday comic strips, which were in color, across the inside of the shoebox openings. The end result looked like stained glass windows when small candles placed in the boxes were lit. The shoebox lid was not used so that the box would not catch on fire during the parade. We tied a stout piece of string to one end of the box to be used as a pull rope. When it was dark the candles were lit and we paraded single file around the block dragging the lighted boxes behind us for all the neighbors to see. We knew that everyone sat out on their front porches to cool off during those hot, humid Indiana summer evenings.

Almost every house in our neighborhood had a front porch swing, used mainly for sitting and socializing with the neighbors. A few hardy souls slept out on the porch on hot nights as well. In the early evening, neighbors often walked by our house on their way to the corner drugstore, perhaps to buy a double-dip ice cream cone or a fountain Coke which only cost ten cents each. After a friendly wave, the neighbors might walk up to our porch, linger for a chat, and get caught up on the local gossip. The fact that none of the houses had air conditioning encouraged everyone to sit outside to cool off. There were no televisions or computers enticing us to stay inside. If we wanted to listen to a favorite radio show, we simply turned on the inside radio, opened a living room window and let the sound find us on the front porch.

During the summer months younger boys and girls in our Park Avenue neighborhood played together outside from dawn to dusk. Some of our favorite games as youngsters were Statues, Red Light-Green Light, Mother May I? and games of hide-and-seek such as Tappy on the Icebox and Kick the Can. Those games were played until it was almost dark when the porch lights went on as a signal for kids to return home. At that point, whoever was "it" yelled at the top of their voice Olly, Olly Oxen, all in freeee!

A game that boys learned to play at an early age was marbles, or Ringer as it was called. The game had its own language. During the game you heard words used like taw, trolley, ducks, miggs, fudging, histing, lofting, dubs, picks, and mibster. The only requirements to play were a bag of marbles and a steady hand and eye. A three to five foot circle was roughed out in the dirt as the playing field. Then each player put an equal number of marbles in the center of the circle. Of course we generally played with the cheaper nondescript glass marbles and kept the cats-eyes and agates for collecting or trading. Pee-wees were usually kept out of the game. They were irregularly shaped, smaller, cheap clay marbles and were looked upon with contempt. The object of the game was for the shooter to knock as many of his opponent's marbles as he could out of the circle without missing. The shooter used a large one-inch diameter glass marble while the marbles in play were usually about ½ inch in diameter. If the first shooter knocked out one or more on the first try, he continued shooting until he missed. Then the next player had his try. Whoever took home more marbles than he came with was declared a winner.

Like many other children's games, the marble game rules varied by neighborhood. We didn't use any written rules and had no umpires, referees, coaches, or official arbitrators. The rules were hammered out in the heat of battle. There were endless discussions and arguments over some of the finer points of the game. For example, what was the proper and permitted way to hold the shooter marble? Was it to be knuckles down, and if so was the palm of the hand to be flush with the ground, or could it be raised to give more leverage and striking power? The real problem came with the arrival of a player from another neighborhood (the next block). He might want to use a "steelie" as a shooter. If allowed, the results could be devastating. The "steelie" was a large, heavy, steel ball bearing. If it hit the cluster of lightweight glass marbles in the center of the circle, they scattered like leaves in the wind. One of our neighborhood rules was that "steelies" were not allowed in the game.

The main co-ed activity in our backyard, as elsewhere in our neighborhood, was the hotly contested game of poison croquet. We had grown tired of the more conventional game of croquet that had its roots in ancient Gaul. From there the game had spread to Buckingham Palace in England and finally to America in the early 1800s. The game of poison is a variation of the croquet game called Rover, in which the first player to complete the course without hitting the final stake leaves his ball in play to help his partner complete the course. In the game of poison, the first player to complete the course was designated as poisoner. He then roamed the playing field to knock other players out of the game by hitting their ball with his poison ball. If all went well and his aim was good, the poisoner was the last player left on the course. To be declared the winner, he had to hit the finish stake with his last shot from wherever his ball was in play. Failing to hit the stake meant no winner that time.

Of course during the game of poison croquet it was expected that the younger boys and girls would nudge their ball from time to time.

Nudging often took place when it was difficult for the youngster to hit the ball through the wire wicket in one shot which was called being "wired." A quick side kick, when no one else was supposedly looking, is all it took to move the ball into proper playing position. This type of cheating was tolerated in the younger players.

In our early teen-age years we boys became fascinated with kite flying. The first harbinger of spring in our neighborhood was a sky filled with kites. Just as the strong March winds began to blow, we hurried over to the corner drugstore to purchase our kites. We seldom had the luxury of using a prior year's kite, since more often than not their skeletal remains hung for several months from tall trees in our neighborhood. If the corner drugstore had run out of the Hi-Flyer kite, we rode our bikes to Danner Brothers in downtown Broad Ripple to purchase one. The Hi-Flyer was our favorite since it was inexpensive, easily assembled, and was emblazoned with the image of an early model airplane. While at Danner Brothers we also purchased a large quantity of strong kite string.

We begged our mothers for old sheets that we tore into thin strips for kite tails, to help stabilize the kite in the air. Our favorite place for kite flying was the street in front of our house. It was a real challenge, because it took a great deal of skill to keep the kites out of the tall trees that bordered our street.

Kites have been a part of our history for several hundred years. As early as 1700 kites were used in Scotland as weather spotters when thermometers were attached to them. There is the famous story of Benjamin Franklin, who in 1789 ran out into an electrical storm and launched his kite to determine the relationship between electricity and lightning. In 1894 Sir Baden Powell, founder of the Boy Scouts, lifted a man off the ground attached to a thirty-six foot long kite. Kites were also used by the French military for signaling purposes as far back as the Franco-Prussian War, and by our U.S. Weather Bureau for observation purposes as late as the 1930s.

By our middle teens we boys expanded our interest in sports to football and basketball, both of which were very popular at high school. For football, we used the street in front of our house as a playground. For some unknown reason Park Avenue was quite a bit wider in our block than south of us. A three-foot strip of the old paving bricks on each side of the street is still visible at curbside. The bricks were similar to the ones used to pave the Indianapolis Motor Speedway in 1909. That project required 3.2 million paving bricks that were primarily supplied by the Wabash Clay Company of Veedersburg, IN. Most of those bricks are still embedded in the Indianapolis Motor Speedway track lying underneath several inches of asphalt paving.

As older teenagers, we enjoyed playing the game of Pass and Kick Football. The object of the game was to advance the ball past the opposing team's goal line. Whichever team could consistently kick or pass the ball farthest won the game.

Basketball was played at the home of any friend who was fortunate enough to have a hoop mounted on his garage roof. As teenagers our favorite basketball game was called Horse. The advantage of the game was that any number of boys could play, since each player was on his own. Whenever a player made a bucket, the next shooter had to make the same shot. If he missed the shot, he received a letter starting with H. If he made the same shot as the first shooter, the next player in sequence had to make the shot with the same consequences. This rotation continued until someone missed the shot. Then the next player started a new round by trying to make a different basket. If a player missed five shots he was "awarded" a total of five letters (H-O-R-S-E) and was out of the game. The game continued until only one player was left with less than five letters.

It seems as if there was always something happening in our neighborhood during the Depression. A real treat for boys and girls during the warm summer months was the arrival of the iceman from the Broad Ripple Ice Company. Several of the houses on our block didn't have electric refrigerators, relying instead on wooden iceboxes for keeping food and drink cool. Since Dad worked for Westinghouse Electric, we had the luxury of owning an electric refrigerator early on. Every house on the iceman's route had a requisite cardboard sign in the front window. The way the sign was positioned let the driver know how much ice, if any, the housewife wanted that day. The driver climbed up on the bed of the truck and chipped off the requested amount, typically a twenty-five or fifty pound block. He then placed a thick leather pad over his shoulder and with a pair of ice tongs heaved the large block of ice onto the pad. While he was carrying the ice to the house, we children scrambled onto the truck bed, looking for small slivers of ice. On a hot day, sucking on a piece of ice was a "cool treat," long before Dairy Queen used that phrase in their advertising.

As young kids we seldom missed the arrival of the mailman since we spent most of our days outside during the summer and on weekends. The mailman was typically male, white, and in our opinion very old—at least forty. We called him Uncle Sam and always hoped for a piece of personal mail that seldom came. In those days mail was delivered twice daily, in the morning and in the afternoon. Perhaps mail then meant more than it does today since then there was no junk mail. Even the Sears catalog had to be picked up at their retail store in downtown Indianapolis, now a small Marsh supermarket. Our family's usual daily mail was a piece or two of personal or business correspondence, maybe a utility bill and perhaps a postcard from one of the local department stores announcing a forthcoming sale. Back then the three main types of long distance communication were the telegram, telephone, and U.S. mail. Since the first two types were too expensive for most of us, our parents engaged in the now lost art of letter writing.

I still treasure that first piece of personal mail I ever received back in 1937. The card even had my own name written on the front. I had written a letter to Santa Claus several days earlier, and much to my surprise he wrote me back. His penny postcard said that he had received my letter and the toys I had asked for were at Block's Department store in downtown Indianapolis. More importantly, Santa's note said that I could see him in person at Block's. Never in my wildest dreams would I have guessed he lived at Block's Department Store in my very own town. The next year I received an even more impressive piece of mail. It was a picture postcard from a real foreign country— Canada. An older neighborhood friend, Bob Buckler, sent me the card when his family visited Niagara Falls, Ontario, and New York City. What was even more thrilling was his personal note saying that he was bringing me back a souvenir of his trip—three comic books.

A few years later Bob gave me something that I also treasured for a long time. It was my first wallet. No matter that it was his cast off—old, worn and soiled. None of my friends carried a billfold as pre-teenagers but now I did and it made me feel older and more important; now I was somebody. I desperately wanted to put something in the wallet as I certainly didn't have any folding money. All of my fortune was in loose change in my piggy bank. However I did own a lucky Indian head penny which I put in the wallet. I also put in my official Cub Scout membership card which had my name and address for all to see. In addition I included my membership cards in the Sons of the American Legion and Captain Midnight's Secret Squad. Something was still missing; I needed a photograph of girl of about my age which I could pass off as a girlfriend. Fortunately I found a suitable picture in our family photograph album. The young girl was the daughter of a family friend who had moved out of town several years earlier. Her photograph had been sent to my parents to show how much she had grown in the interim. It didn't matter that I had never met her in person. I placed her picture in my wallet's glassine window hoping that one of the guys would ask to see her picture but they never did. It's too bad since I had a great story to tell about our supposed friendship.

One of the most memorable events at our house was the arrival of the coal truck. Mary Ellen and I were fascinated with the process of moving coal from the truck parked at curbside to our coal bin door on the side of the house. First the coal man constructed a ramp with wooden planks from the front sidewalk to the narrow walkway that led around the house to our side yard. Next the driver put in place a portable steel coal chute that reached from the ground level door opening down to the basement coal bin floor. Then the driver shoveled the coal out of the truck bed into a heavy wheelbarrow and pushed it from the street to the side of our house. The coal was then dumped into the chute where it slid down into the bin. Periodically the deliveryman had to go into the basement to reposition the coal. After he was finished, he always left his calling card, a thick layer of black coal dust on the front and side walkway leading to the coal bin door. The residual effects of burning high sulfur Indiana coal in Indianapolis furnaces included the pungent smell of sulfur in the winter air and the black coating of soot that always appeared on new fallen snow and on washing left out too long on the clothesline.

In summer, the arrival of the ice cream truck in our neighborhood was always a big treat. We eagerly awaited the distant sound of his tinkling bells as we played outside. That gave us enough time to run inside and try to beg a nickel or dime from Mom. If all else failed, we pried the necessary coins out of our piggy banks. Then we had to make the difficult choice between an Eskimo Pie, Fudge Bar, Cream-sicle, Popsicle or that little ice cream sundae served in a paper cup. My favorite treat was the Popsicle, because the wrappers could be saved and mailed in for small prizes.

As pre-schoolers Mary Ellen and I also looked forward to the daily arrival of the Freihofer Bakery truck. Along with deliveries of tasty baked goods, every Monday the driver had the latest copy of the Nip & Tuck Weekly. The handout was a four-page booklet of stories, cartoons and a page to color. The best part of all was that Nip & Tuck was free.

Also delivered daily were dairy products from the Polk Sanitary Milk Company. Mom usually left a note in one of the empty milk bottles on the front porch to let the milkman know what was needed that day. The bottles were housed in a small metal storage box that was embossed with the Polk logo, which was the head of a Guernsey cow and the saying "Polk's Milk, Always Ahead." In the early 1930s the dairy switched from horse drawn vehicles to a fleet of Stutz motor-ized Pak-age-Cars manufactured in Indianapolis.

In the 1930s, out of necessity there were many self-employed men who either sold items door to door or offered some type of house-hold service, such as simple home repairs and window washing. One popular event was the appearance of the summer vegetable huckster. The old Model A Ford huckster wagon was driven slowly down the middle of the street by one man, while his partner walked along the sidewalk, yelling at the top of his voice, "CORN, BEANS AND TO-MATOES FOR SALE!"

Another popular vendor was the door-to-door photographer whose prospective customers were families with young children. He brought with him a pony, a box camera with tripod, and a cowboy costume consisting of a hat, bandana, and chaps. For a small fee he photographed the young would-be cowboy sitting on his pony. The photo was printed right there. I had my chance, at the age of seven, to be photographed as a rough and ready cowboy. I always wondered how the pony and photographer arrived in our neighborhood, as I saw no sign of a truck or car. Perhaps the man had ridden the pony into town from his house in the country or maybe the man lived down the street and housed his pony in his garage or back yard.

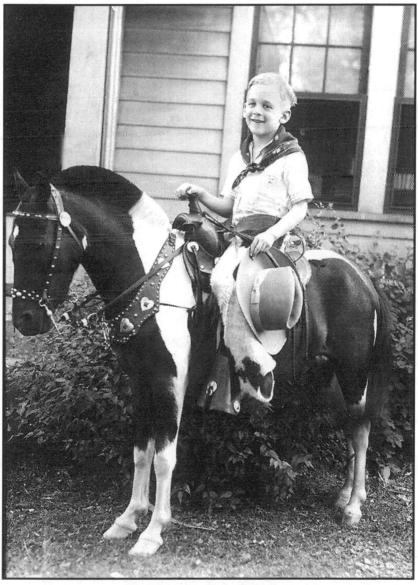

COWBOY DESPERADO

In the depths of the Depression, it was not uncommon for a poorly dressed man to knock on our door and ask if there were any odd jobs that he could do for a meal or a small handout. One of the more enterprising men carried number stencils and a small can of black paint and a brush with him. When we answered his knock at the door, he asked if we wanted our street address numbers painted on the front curb in exchange for a little cash.

Another door-to-door vendor was the knife and scissors sharpener. He carried a small but heavy grinding wheel tied to a rope and slung over his shoulder. I always wondered how he could get enough business to make a living.

The most popular door-to-door peddler over the years was the notions man. I found out many years later that his name was Herbie Wirth. He toted two heavy paper shopping bags filled with an amazing array of small household items, ranging from wash cloths to whisk brooms. The one item that I most remember were those bright pink, evil smelling deodorizers that were hung over the rim of the toilet bowl. Although Herbie's visits were infrequent because of the large north side area he covered, we all came to know him over the twenty-four years he walked door to door in our neighborhood. I could never have guessed that one day he would have a feature article written about him in the July 1971 issue of *Readers Digest* magazine. It turned out that Herbie had no family or close friends when he passed away suddenly. When his former customers found out about his passing, they started making telephone calls around town. Soon the word was out, and when Herbie's funeral was held on a cold winter's day in February 1971 at Crown Hill Cemetery, over one thousand people attended.

All of the kids in our neighborhood knew everyone by name from the corner store merchants to the families on our block. There was the barber John Sanders, the druggist Henry Silver, the grocer Amos Pedigo, and the service station owner Shotzy. In addition to their names, we knew where most of the neighbors worked. For example, on our block of twenty five houses we kids knew that Russell Stubbs was a professional musician who played the saxophone in a local dance band, Norman Brady owned a scrap yard and had family interests in a local supper club, John Carpenter was actually a carpenter by trade,

Paul Buckler was the chief teller at the downtown headquarters of Indiana National Bank, John Scott was a purchasing agent for Eli Lilly & Co., Gus Rosen was president of Rock Wool Insulators, Aaron Dee owned Dee Jewelry Co., Eli Ettinger was treasurer at Leon Tailoring Co., Eugene Barnhill was general manager of Indianapolis Wire Bound Box Co., Lawrence Eaton was a home builder, and Fred McComb was a captain in the U.S. Army who worked at the Finance Center at nearby Ft. Benjamin Harrison.

None of the wives in our neighborhood worked outside of the house. As a result, they frequently had friends over for a visit during the day. Whenever I saw women walking up to our next door neighbor's house, I knew that Rose Rosen was having friends in for an afternoon of Mah Jong. Other afternoons I saw Mary Stubs, who lived across the street from us, sunbathing in the front yard with one of her younger girl friends. The two of them spent hours in the sun in their canvas sling deck chairs. They were usually outfitted in quite daring two piece bathing suits. It was during this period of my growing up that I honed my ogling skills to a true art form.

No one in our neighborhood had a spacious house, and yet there was often a doubling up of families. The returning World War II veterans finding no place for their families to live were often forced to move in with one or the other set of parents. This was due to the extreme housing shortage as a result of the Great Depression and WW II. Because of economic or practical circumstances, a maiden aunt or elderly grandparent often became part of the family household. There were few if any retirement homes or extended care facilities, except for the county poor farms.

Although most of the typical family units in our neighborhood consisted of a father, mother and one to three children, it was not unusual to find larger families with three generations living under one roof or families with several children. For example, the O'Connor family had eight children, all with good Irish names: Maureen, Kathleen, Sharlene, Timothy, Michael etc. The other large family unit, the Bolles, also had eight children.

My playmate Frank Marsella lived in the next block with his extended family. Over time, his two-story house held Frank and his younger brother, his mother and father, his grandmother and grandfather, a married aunt and uncle and two single uncles who stayed there on the weekends. They all seemed to get along fine, but I did wonder where everybody slept in that house. I envied them in a way, because my family had no relatives living in the state, much less under one roof in our own house. I thought it would be neat to just walk down the stairs from my bedroom to visit with one of my grandparents, instead of having a five-hour drive to their home in Chicago.

Our neighborhood was quite stable, as people seldom moved in or out. Most of our neighbors were there when we moved into our Park Avenue house in 1937 and were still there when we moved out in 1951; however there were some exceptions. A few of the modest bungalows on our block seemed to serve merely as way stations for the upwardly mobile. Those families stayed in our neighborhood for a year or two and then moved a few blocks west to one of the larger houses on Washington Boulevard, Pennsylvania, or Meridian Streets.

An example of an upwardly mobile family was the Bradys, who moved in directly across the street from our house. Their extended family owned scrap metal operations and several taverns and restaurants, including the Red Gables at 16th Street and Lafayette Road. We wondered about them when they first moved in because Mr. Brady drove a brand new, fancy 1948 Cadillac. He always parked the car in front of his house overnight, rather than in his garage off the rear alley. We wondered if his car was too large to fit in that small garage, or if he just wanted to make a statement to the neighbors. No one else in the neighborhood owned a Cadillac, new or used, or for that matter any new car. When we parked our 1933 Buick across the street from his 1948 Cadillac, the difference in economic status was glaringly obvious. Sure enough, within a year or two the Brady family moved into one of those large, fancy houses over on Pennsylvania Street.

NEIGHBORHOOD CHARACTERS

As with other neighborhoods, ours had its share of eccentrics. Across the street from our second rental house lived Old Lady Harless who was employed by a lingerie company to go door to door selling women's unmentionables. She was a single, older, short, stout woman with no discernible figure. Her face looked as if it had been sprayed with a wrinkle gun. To try and hide the wrinkles she covered it in a layer of crimson rouge and a thick dusting of powder. I remember her lingering in front of the retail shops at the corner of 54th and College. On more than one occasion Miss Harless confronted an unsuspecting lady she had never seen before and said "Madam, you look like you could use a Spencer corset." Needless to say she didn't sell many corsets that way, although there was a market for them at the time when the hourglass figure was in vogue.

Miss Harless took in a boarder during the Depression to help supplement her meager income. We called her boarder Three Fingers Lena because she was missing two fingers from her left hand. Lena worked behind the soda fountain counter at the corner Haag's Drug Store where one of her duties was to prepare the ham salad for the noontime rush. I still remember her cranking the handle of that meat grinder with her right hand and feeding freshly cooked chunks of ham into it with her left hand. I always wondered if she lost her two fingers in that grinder.

Another neighborhood character was an older man we called the crazy dentist. He lived a couple of blocks away in a small garage that had been converted into living quarters. In those days most garages were constructed to hold just one car. We children thought that only rich families needed two-car garages. The garages were deliberately constructed on the back property lines facing the alley. All of the streets in our area had alleys behind the houses, eliminating the need for front or side driveways. The advantage of having alleys was that on collection day, trash was piled there and not in front of houses where it was sure to be an eyesore. With no driveways or large garages attached to the front of the houses, the entire front yard could be landscaped into an attractive street view.

Back to the crazy dentist. He drove a vintage Pierce Arrow sedan that he had hand painted a bilious green. The car had two empty front fender wells that provided even more room to stow the cast-off items that he collected from alleys on trash day. In the summer he picked cherries from trees in the neighborhood and went door to door trying to sell them to housewives for pies and cobblers or for canning. Unfortunately for his sales, he carried the cherries in a large chamber pot, which was not too appetizing! We never did know his real name or whether he really had been a dentist at one time.

One of our scarier neighbors was Mrs. Walker who lived in the next block. She frequently walked to the corner shops carrying a large shopping bag. The only thing in the bag was a brick. More often than not, she verbally accosted one of the female sales clerks or shoppers for no apparent reason and threatened to hit her on the head with the brick. As far as I know she was all talk and no action. In the 1930s there was no need to mainstream people with mental problems, since many of them were never institutionalized in the first place. They were thought of as merely being "touched in the head" or had "bats in the belfry."

The two spinster sisters who lived three doors away were also considered different because they drove what we kids thought was a strange automobile. It was powered by electricity. I didn't realize at the time that their car was quite practical for older ladies. Since it ran on electric storage batteries, it didn't produce any noxious fumes, as early gasoline powered cars often did. Also, there was no need to hand crank the electric car to get it started, a task usually required in near zero weather for gasoline vehicles manufactured in the twenties and early thirties. Hand cranking was a tedious chore at best. The sisters' electric car was an old Pope-Waverly that was manufactured in Indianapolis between 1898 and 1916.

Over one hundred different makes of motor vehicle were manufactured in this city between the years 1896 and 1964. The most famous makes were the Marmon, the Duesenberg, and the Stutz. By nineteen hundred the electric car had captured almost forty percent of the automobile market. However, the introduction of the electric starter by Cadillac in 1913 was the beginning of the end for electric cars. Also, due to their short battery charge, electric cars were not practical for long distance driving which became more popular as inter-city roads and highways became more prevalent.

Our move to the new Park Avenue neighborhood in 1937 introduced us to a new set of characters. I remember Mr. Homer Wilson, who was a quiet, mild-mannered, frugal, bespectacled father of two of my playmates. He was also a devout Presbyterian, who wouldn't even purchase a newspaper on the Sabbath since he considered it an inappropriate activity for the day. One neighborhood rumor started when Mr. Wilson pulled his car up in front of his bungalow late one day after work. It was raining very hard with no let-up in sight, and Mr. Wilson had not taken his umbrella to work that morning. After a long wait, he carefully removed his freshly pressed suit coat and trousers, folded them neatly, tucked them under his arm, and ran into the house clothed in his under shorts and white shirt and tie flapping in the breeze. He knew that if his suit was soaked it would cost thirty-five cents to have it pressed at the nearby Scheefer's Dry Cleaners.

Elderly Grandma Wineman was also the talk of the block. On warm sunny days, she sat on her front porch in her rocking chair and smoked a corncob pipe. I was shocked since I had never seen a woman smoke a cigarette before, much less any kind of pipe. It is true that I did enjoy the *Li'l Abner* comic strip in which Mammy Yokum smoked a corncob pipe. As far as cigarettes were concerned, the only women I knew of who smoked were fancy movie stars like Myrna Loy and Bette Davis. Myrna Loy, in the role of Nora Charles in the *Thin Man* movie series always smoked when she went nightclubbing with her husband Nick. As soon as she was seated in the club, she took a long cigarette holder out of her purse. When Nora inserted a Fatima in the holder, Nick gallantly pulled out his gold lighter and lit her cigarette. Nora then took a slow, deep drag and blew out a fancy smoke ring. Boy, was she something!

Old Lady Schenzel lived alone in a small bungalow next to the alley. She seldom ventured outside except to trim her privet hedge with a bread knife. One summer day as I was walking by she asked if I would run an errand to the drug store to pick up her cough medicine. Since a tip was mentioned, I was happy to do as she asked. As instructed, I walked the two blocks to Silver's Pharmacy and asked for the druggist, Henry Silver. When I mentioned her name he handed me a small bottle wrapped in brown paper. Sure enough when I handed Mrs. Schenzel the package, she gave me a dime tip. I guessed that she must have had a severe cough since this errand became a daily routine. It wasn't until a couple of years later while working at Silver's Pharmacy that I discovered I had been faithfully handing her a small bottle of Virginia Dare port wine every day.

A BULLY GOOD TIME

In the good old days almost every neighborhood had a bully-in-residence, and our neighborhood was no exception. The only good thing about bully Bobby Wharton was that he lived at the far end of our long block and around the corner. Fortunately, I didn't need to pass by his house to walk to school or to the corner shops. Bobby had a toady, Ronald Farley, who also lived on our block and acted as his sidekick. Ronald was a conscientious bully trainee and never missed a chance to volunteer for active duty. Bobby was one year older than I, short, heavy set and mean clear through. Word on the street was that Bobby's mother had been a professional wrestler. I am not sure if it was so but I was told that she did have cauliflower ears. Bobby did have an older brother Gene who fortunately kept him in line most of the time. I never—never ventured down to that end of the block. To do so meant possible death or at least severe injury.

From time to time Bobby and his sidekick Ronald roamed the neighborhood looking for trouble. Their most popular forms of torture were the Dutch rub and the "twist the arm behind the back until the victim says uncle" scenario. The Dutch rub consisted of Bobby first grabbing the victim around the neck and bending him over in a headlock. Then he rubbed the knuckles of his closed fist against the victim's head in a circular motion until he grew tired of the sport. When he was feeling magnanimous, Bobby allowed his toady Ronald to do the follow-up arm twisting. Of course Bobby was right there to make sure that Ronald did it properly. I always wondered whose uncle I was pleading with when my arm was twisted behind my back. Was it Bobby's uncle or my uncle? Maybe it was Uncle Sam. Who knows? If these types of torture didn't produce the desired pain and abject terror on the part of the victim, the bullies moved on to the ultimate degradation known as "The Classic Wrist Burn." The bully grabbed a wrist of the victim and twisted it with both hands in opposite directions until he was a quivering mass of fear and suffering.

One day when I had mistakenly lowered my defenses, Bobby ambushed me in the alley and shot me in the foot with his BB gun. Fortunately I was wearing shoes at the time which prevented the possibility of a permanent limp. A few years later, Bobby became a football star at Broad Ripple High School and not surprisingly lived up to his neighborhood reputation.

HEARD ON THE GRAPEVINE

In those days the neighborhood grapevine was an effective way for mothers to monitor their children's activities away from home. Mothers were the eyes and ears of the neighborhood. It was not unusual to be met at the front door by Mom and be admonished for some mischief I had just gotten into several houses away. Our neighborhood was like an extended family. During the day, wives and mothers spent most of the time at home. More often than not, one or more of them was out on the porch, in the yard or walking to a nearby store. As a result, there was usually an adult around to keep an eye on us. If one of us children got out of line, there was a quick telephone call to the kid's mother. We boys and girls also used the neighborhood grapevine to pass along rumors which were always accepted at face value.

Neighborhood rumor had it that my friend Frank Marsella was related to Two-Ton Tony Galento, the infamous heavyweight boxer. Of course I never asked Frank if it was true; you just didn't do that. It was more fun just to think that it might be true. At the tender age of eight I didn't know anybody who knew anybody who was the least bit famous. Tony, a real mauler, finally was granted a heavyweight boxing match with the champ, Joe Louis, on June 28, 1939. Tony actually knocked Louis down in round three but was put out of commission by Louis in round four. All of the neighborhood boys followed Joe Louis' boxing career from the time we were six years old when he became heavyweight champ. We listened to many of his fights on our Westinghouse radio. The only other fighter we were interested in was Tony Zale, the Man of Steel. Tony, whose real name was Anthony Zaleski, was born and raised in Gary, Indiana. After a stint working at the steel mills he became a professional boxer. By 1941 he had become the world middleweight champion. His three championship fights with Rocky Graziano in 1946-48 are considered among the greatest boxing matches ever waged. His 1947 fight with Rocky was witnessed by forty thousand people in Yankee Stadium.

Besides the supposed Two-Ton Tony connection, other rumors swirled around the Park Avenue neighborhood as well. We heard that Louis Zink's father had been a professional wrestler while serving in the U.S. Navy and that Kathleen O'Connor's mother had been an Irish princess and that her father was a real judge. We were also led to believe that a druggist at one of our corner drug stores was a dope fiend and that a neighbor, Mr. Harley, stood in the middle of the street in the dead of night with his pet cat draped around his neck and howled at the moon. Mr. Harley perhaps took his queue or had been influenced by a women's clothing fashion of that era. At that time it was considered quite elegant for a lady to be seen in public wearing a fur scarf around her neck. The fur was usually a fox, rabbit or mink pelt. Whenever a woman walked by wearing one of them I still remember the haunting eyes of those forlorn animals staring down at me as if they were saying "I don't like it up here, I want to roam free in the forest."

Soon after World War II had ended, our neighborhood grapevine was humming with the news that a famous movie actress was coming to Indianapolis. In fact it was said that she would be staying overnight two blocks from our house. During her long film career she was to star in many classics such as the *Dead End Kids; Feudin', Fussin' and A-Fightin'; Ma and Pa Kettle Down on the Farm;* and Indiana's own *Friendly Persuasion.* Of course I am talking about that not so glamorous Hoosier movie star, Marjorie Main. At the time her brother, Samuel J. Tomlinson, lived at 5311 N. College Avenue. When we learned that Miss Main would be visiting so close to home, my sister and I decided to try and get her autograph. With our autograph books in hand and with some trepidation, we walked over to her brother's house. Her movie roles had always portrayed her as a rather severe, plain looking woman with that rusty nail voice, who was always worried about something or other. It was hard to believe that much earlier in life she was a charter member of Delta Delta Delta sorority at Indiana's Franklin College. When we knocked on the door of that humble bungalow, much to our surprise she was quite friendly, invited us in for a chat, and was happy to sign our autograph books.

Today if you drive through my old neighborhood very slowly, open the driver's side window and listen very carefully, you can faintly hear some of those rumors still floating through the air like a soft summer breeze

THOSE CORNER SHOPS

The corner shops at 54th and College were just two blocks from our home. At the corner there were two pharmacies-Silver's and Haag's Drugs; two grocery stores- Pedigo's and Krogers; two service stations-Chotzen Pure Oil and Enarco; two barber shops-Saunders and Clarks; two dry cleaners-Scheefers and Center; and two restaurants including Scotten's Cafeteria. In addition, there were several other small retail shops, one of which was a dry goods store. If an item couldn't be found there, the family usually found it at one of the many larger Broad Ripple retail shops. For us kids, Broad Ripple village was the real downtown, since those stores had everything we could possibly want. With such a wide variety of stores so close to home, my parents seldom needed to venture to downtown Indianapolis to shop at the three large department stores.

While living on Carrollton Avenue, I remember making frequent trips to nearby Pedigo's Grocery Store with Mom and Mary Ellen. In the 1930s and early 1940s, most housewives in our neighborhood didn't know how to drive, so they walked every day or two to the nearest grocery store to purchase perishables and other food items. It is somewhat ironic that Mom never learned to drive, since her father had been a chauffeur for the private Chicago Club in the Windy City for many years. After our move to the house on Park Avenue, we continued to purchase most of our groceries at Pedigo's. Mom usually pulled my empty wagon to the grocery store and returned home loaded with grocery sacks.

Pedigo's Grocery Store had a large adjoining vacant lot that ran between College Ave. and the alley. This was a great place to explore. One day a kid uncovered some bones while digging for "buried treasure." All of us were excited that something sinister had transpired. It was later determined that the find was just a bunch of old dog bones. Then there was a rumor that the vacant lot would be converted into an outdoor theater. As children we had visions of seeing free movies, perhaps from our own back yard. Of course the rumor had no basis in fact. The vacant lot was certainly not large enough for an outdoor theater even if zoning laws had allowed it to be built. The first drive-in movie theater in Indianapolis, the Pendleton Pike, opened soon thereafter in 1940. In the 1930s there was a small diner on Pedigo's property along College Avenue called Hink and Dink's owned by Vernal Hinkel. On the rare occasion when I had lunch there as a special treat, I remember hamburger steaks were fifteen cents and Coca-Colas were five cents.

Another treat for us younger boys and girls was a visit to the corner drugstore for penny candy. We first needed to pry a few pennies from our piggy banks. If we were really lucky we might free up a buffalo head nickel. In those days, children were often given small savings banks by their parents to instill the virtue of thrift. That was no doubt in part due to the lingering Depression. The banks typically came in three styles. The most popular was in the shape of a pig and made of china. The only way to remove the coins was to smash the pig, a day Mary Ellen and I looked forward to. A second type of bank, usually made of thin metal, required a key to open. The coin slot was cleverly designed as a one-way only deposit slot. Of course our parents hid the key where we couldn't find it, although we certainly looked everywhere. The third type of bank was cast iron and came in various shapes and sizes. My bank was in the form of a two-story house but there was no apparent way to open it. I never understood the rationale for putting money in a bank that could never be opened. The coin retrieval system was so complicated that we kids remained permanently baffled. To this day I still save all of my change in a piggy bank, except that my current bank is bright yellow plastic in the shape of a honey bear. Its main advantage is that I can easily twist off the plastic lid anytime I need change.

When we arrived at the drugstore with coins in hand, we were in seventh heaven. There were so many choices of penny candy: Jelly beans, B-B Bats, Guess What's, Tootsie rolls, gum drops, red and black licorice whips, small wax bottles filled with a colored sweet liquid, Double Bubble gum, jaw breakers, Red Hots and lollipops. Thank goodness no one talked about cavities, calories, cholesterol or carbohydrates. My favorite candy was the Guess-What which in addition to two pieces of salt-water taffy, included in every package a cartoon in color printed on heavy waxed paper.

The most coveted and forbidden penny treat was the infamous Horrors of War card and bubble gum. For a penny we could purchase a flat three-inch square piece of bubble gum. The gum wasn't as important as the accompanying card illustrating a war scene of the time in graphic color. The cards were first issued in 1938, before our country's entry into World War II. As has always been true even to this day, the producers, Gum, Inc. had several wars to select from, such as Italy's invasion of Ethiopia in 1935, the Spanish Civil War in 1936, or the Chinese-Japanese War of 1937. Several of the cards in the series are still emblazoned in my mind. The more graphic cards depicted what might have happened to civilians in those war torn countries when an enemy bomb or shell exploded in their midst. Those cards showed various body parts flying through the air in living color.

HORRORS OF WAR GUM CARD
ITALY BOMBS ETHIOPIA–1935

My parents heard about that set of cards through the neighborhood grapevine and forbade me to buy them. They thought I might become traumatized with all of that blood and gore. Personally I thought the cards were keen. However, taking my parents literally, I didn't buy any of the cards. I merely traded for them, using comic books as currency. I was always afraid that one day Dad or Mom might search my bedroom to look for the forbidden goods. This type of search happened all the time in the Big House, as heard on one of my favorite radio programs, *Gangbusters,* but my parents never found anything. Perhaps that is because I hid anything I didn't want them to find in my next door neighbor's outside basement window well. Whenever I wanted my contraband, their window well was only a few feet away from our side walkway.

As far as bubble gum itself was concerned, my favorite was Fleer's Double Bubble Gum. The large wad of pink gum came with an inside wrapper of waxy paper. On the paper was printed a cartoon in color and your personal fortune. We had contests to see who could blow the biggest bubble without bursting it. Some of us tried to gain a competitive advantage by cramming several pieces in our mouths at one time. Chewing that large mass of gum, we were not unlike our elders with their Mail Pouch Chewing Tobacco, although we did no spitting. The most fun was when someone blew an extraordinarily large bubble and it exploded. The blower ended up with a pink facemask that had to be removed with care. Any classmate at grade school bold enough to chew bubble gum during class was considered quite daring. If caught, he had to remove the gum from his mouth and stick it on the bridge of his nose for the remainder of the class period.

From time to time on Saturday mornings Dad drove us to the one of the few so-called super markets in the area, the A & P (Atlantic & Pacific Tea Company) located on 38th Street near College Avenue. It was a real family event, with Mary Ellen and me looking forward to acquiring some of our four major food groups: candy, cake, cookies, and custard. Most appealing were the sample food displays. I could eat almost enough to qualify as a meal, between the cheese cubes on toothpicks and the dill pickle slices sitting on top of a large wooden barrel. Often I sampled snack foods that were found in unsealed packages. I assumed that the wrappers were torn due to rough handling and that the contents were up for grabs. My sister accused me of opening sealed packages on purpose, just so I could sample them. Not guilty!

The other grocery stores of any size in our neighborhood were the Stop & Shop at the corner of 56th and Illinois St. and the Standard Grocery Store and the A & P in Broad Ripple. We rarely went to any of those markets, since they didn't offer as wide a selection as the 38th Street A & P. As a kid I wondered if the A & P and the Stop and Shop market chains had merged, would they call the newly named stores Stop and P

On The Go

BIKES AND OTHER WHEELS

During my tenth birthday party, I endured the ritual birthday spanking in which the guests gave me the ten mandatory swats with "one extra to grow on." What helped ease the pain was the neat present my parents had given me earlier in the day; my first regulation full-size bicycle. It was a sparkling, shiny, cream and maroon Schwinn bicycle. No other make would do. To us boys, the Schwinn was the Cadillac of bicycles. We couldn't be bothered with the Shelby, the American Flyer, the Hawthorne, the Mercury, or the J.C. Higgins. The Schwinn arrived with all the necessary equipment: white wall tires, chrome handlebars, a genuine leather saddle (seat), a frame tank with built-in horn, a fancy chain guard and a rear luggage carrier. The carrier was quite practical for toting home a box of groceries from the market or for hanging saddlebags that could be used to carry newspapers for delivery. The bike also featured a front fender headlight, fancy rubber handlebar grips and bright red glass reflectors.

For those boys who really wanted to make a statement, the bike could be jazzed up with even more accessories from Broad Ripple Guarantee Auto Supply or Vonnegut Hardware, such as rear view mirrors mounted on the handle bars, speedometers, mud flaps, rear fender ornaments, and red reflector signs with snappy sayings such as "excuse my dust." In the event of a flat tire, a small leatherette tool kit strapped to the back of the bike seat came in handy. The tool kit usually included a tire gauge, a spoke tightening wrench, a tube repair kit and a miniature tire pump. What we didn't use or need was a bike lock. I never heard of anyone having his bike stolen, even if left for several hours in a remote area.

Owning a bicycle gave me the independence I had wanted for such a long time and which is still a trait I value today. No need to walk long distances or wait for the next streetcar, bus, or trackless trolley that didn't take me near where I wanted to go anyway. No bumming a ride on a friend's bike (called trailing). Riding double was not only uncomfortable and dangerous but illegal as well! That Schwinn bike became like a good friend; we were inseparable. I went everywhere on my bike, from downtown Indianapolis to the Indianapolis Motor Speedway to Broad Ripple Park to Riverside Amusement Park to the Riviera Club, to Little America (not the one in the Antarctica), and to the playground at the corner of 61st and Broadway Streets.

My desire to own a bicycle was enhanced by the fact that my close grade and high school chum Dick Rhude had received a new Schwinn bicycle for his birthday earlier that year. I was also influenced by the publicity associated with six-day bike races when I was a youngster. Although the six-day bike race started with the advent of the track safety bike in the 1890s, it became a major sport during the Great Depression. During this period, bikers from many countries raced for large cash prizes on indoor tracks such as Madison Square Garden in New York City and even at the Butler Fieldhouse here in Indianapolis. The riders had their own language, including words such as jumper, hipped, allee, hooking, and pick-up. The men paired up for a series of races over the mandatory six-day period during which one member of the team had to be riding on the track at all times. The riders competed in a series of sprints, with points awarded to the winners. The team winning the most points during the six-day period won the grand cash prize. Typically the winners rode their bikes between two thousand and twenty seven hundred miles during the six-day race. Because of the great need for energy, the riders ate up to ten small meals a day and took catnaps whenever possible throughout the six-day event. The most famous racing stars during the 1930s were the team of Gustave Killian and Heinz Vopel from Germany, who raced in Indianapolis at the Butler Fieldhouse in 1937. It was the first international six-day bike race ever held in this city, with thirty thousand spectators in attendance over the six-day period. Killian and Vopel won the race by accumulating the greatest number of points of the nine teams who competed.

My love affair with my Schwinn bike almost came to a crashing end one day. For some reason I decided to ride my bike back to grade school shortly after closing hours. I parked the bike at curbside across from the school and ran into school for a couple of minutes on an errand. When I came out, someone's car had run over the back wheel of my bike and left the scene. I half wheeled and half carried my mangled bike home. Fortunately Dad, quite the handyman, was able to straighten out the rear frame enough for me to use the bike. The crumpled rear wheel rim was replaced, but something was lost that could never be replaced. It was that feeling which a kid gets when he has something very special of his own like a sharp looking bicycle. Yes, I continued to ride the bike for several more years during the period known as the "strip" years. The cool thing as we got older was to strip all non-functional parts off the bike and replace the stodgy handlebars with racing ones. The bikes were then transformed into lean, mean, pedaling machines, not unlike the dirt bikes of today.

Before joining the Riviera Swim Club, Rhude and I often rode our bikes to Broad Ripple Park to swim. The park featured what was billed as the world's largest outdoor cement bottom pool. It was a great place to play water tag until the lifeguards wised up to our antics. The pool also had a long water slide that we monopolized whenever we could. It did not hurt the pool's reputation that Johnny Weissmuller, the future *Tarzan of the Apes* movie star, had won the hundred meter free-style event there in preparation for the 1924 Olympic meet.

Just down the road from Broad Ripple Park was the Little America amusement park, at the corner of 62nd Street and Keystone Avenue. It was the real Little America, as far as we were concerned, although in school we had learned that in 1928, Admiral Richard Byrd founded an exploration base on the Antarctic continent that he called Little America. Our Little America was a far cry from that cold, desolate terrain. Here we enjoyed several forms of outdoor entertainment, such as pony rides, a carousel, a miniature golf course, a penny arcade, and a golf driving range. Our favorite activity was chasing after misdirected golf balls that had been hit off the two story driving platform. Often the balls went over the high fence that surrounded the fairway and landed along Keystone Avenue for easy pickings. Once I purchased a bucket of golf balls to see what it was like to hit them off the upper deck. Unfortunately on my first attempt, I lost my grip on the club and it went end over end far out into the fairway. The real embarrassment was that the club went farther than the golf ball. I never could get the knack of playing golf, or bowling for that matter. I gave up both sports early on. If only I could have switched my golf and bowling scores. My score in golf was always well over 100 and my score in bowling was usually under 100.

For several years we kids reserved Saturday afternoons for movie watching only. This was an inviolate rule not to be broken at any cost. We had a choice among four theaters on the north side of Indianapolis, all within easy bike riding distance: the Zaring Egyptian at 27th and Central Avenue, the Ritz at 34th and Illinois Street, the Uptown at 42nd and College Avenue, and the Vogue Theater on College Avenue near Broad Ripple Avenue.

The Vogue Theater, nearest our home, was constructed in 1938 and had a gala opening on June 18th of that year. The first movie was "College Swing" starring Martha Raye and Burns (George) and Allen (Gracie). Selling tickets at the first showing were Olsen and Johnson, popular stars of radio, stage and screen. They were appearing in person at the time at the Lyric Theater in downtown Indianapolis in their comedy revue "Hellzapoppin." Like Cole Porter, John (Ole) Olsen was born in Peru, Indiana. Hoagy Carmichael, another Hoosier, scored the music for the movie. Ken Maynard, popular Hoosier cowboy star of the period, had laid the Vogue Theater's cornerstone a few weeks earlier. Like Hollywood Boulevard, the theater had its own mini walk of fame, consisting of a single bronze star that is still embedded in the sidewalk in front of the building. The star was signed for the gala opening by twenty-seven movie stars with Hoosier connections. One of them, Carol Lombard of Ft. Wayne and her husband to be, Clark Gable, were there in person. Included with the star signatures is the following inscription in bronze, "To our Hoosier Friends, Carl Niesse." Niesse was the owner/manager of the Vogue Theater. Of the four north side theaters operating at the time, only the Vogue is still in operation today offering live entertainment rather than conventional movies.

VOGUE THEATER SIDEWALK STAR

Our preteen theater of choice was the Uptown, perhaps because unlike the other theaters they featured a Wurlitzer organ in the early days. We rode our bikes to the theater early every Saturday afternoon. After we paid the eleven-cent admission and bought boxes of popcorn and Milk Duds, we settled down for several hours of entertainment. The bill of fare always included two full length movies, a newsreel of the day, previews of coming attractions, a cartoon, and finally an ongoing weekly serial featuring such heavies as the Cisco Kid or the Green Hornet. At intermission the house lights went up. It was time to restock our candy and popcorn. In addition, it was time for an audience sing along. Lyrics of a popular song were projected on the screen, accompanied by a tune blaring out of the loudspeakers. A small moving white circle appeared above each word as it was to be sung by the audience in time to the recorded music. This became known as a "Follow the Bouncing Ball" sing along.

As a pre-teenager my favorite movie hero was Rin Tin Tin. That seemed like a funny name for a movie actor until I found out he happened to be a German shepherd dog. He was named after the French puppet Rin Tin Tin who was popular before WW I. Rin Tin Tin, the puppy, had been the offspring of a German shepherd who was used for war duty by the Germans in France in 1918. The puppy was discovered by an American soldier in a bombed out French kennel during the war and brought back to the states. Showing exceptional learning skills and alertness, the dog was taken to Hollywood for a tryout in the movies. After a brief role in some movie shorts, the dog was featured in twenty-six Warner Brothers' films and received as many as ten thousand fan letters a week from his adoring fans. Rin Tin Tin was to his fans what the Collie Lassie was to the next generation of kids.

As an older teenager my favorite movie heroes were the Dead End Kids. They were always cast as a gang of teenage juvenile delinquents who lived in Brooklyn during the depths of the Great Depression. Their first movie appearance was in the film *Dead End* staring Humphrey Bogart released in 1937. The cast included Indiana's own Marjorie Main. The movie *Dead End* was a sordid and depressing look at life in New York's poor Lower East Side adapted from a Broadway play of the same name. The Dead End Kids continued to act as juvenile delinquents for another twenty one years and eighty six films. During that period many of the gang members were replaced and their gang moniker segued from the Dead End Kids to the Little Tough Guys to the East Side Boys to the Clancy Street Boys to the Bowery Boys.

My favorite gang member was Leo Gorcey, born in 1917, who had the staying power to star in the gang movies from the first one in 1937 until the middle 1950s. Leo played the part of a tough, short, and not-so-smart rabble rouser who talked out of the side of his mouth and considered a sleeveless undershirt as appropriate outer wear. His gang name was appropriately Muggs. Two of Leo's brothers also served as sometime gang members, David and Billy Gorcey. In 1944 Leo became a regular on the radio program *Blue Ribbon Town* starring

Groucho Marx. This was several years before Groucho's popular TV program *You Bet Your Life*. Leo's job on the radio was to needle Groucho which he did with relish.

When not at the Saturday movies during the summer, we teenage boys assembled at the 61st Street playground with softball mitts in hand. The playground featured a softball diamond that was rarely used by anyone other than neighborhood boys. If there were enough kids, the best players became self-appointed team captains. They took turns selecting teammates until all of us were chosen. If there were too few of us to have two full teams, we played rotation softball. One of the better players acted as captain and assigned the other kids to specific playing positions. Of course, the captain appointed himself leadoff batter and selected his three closest friends as backup hitters. Every time a batter or someone on base was called out, he switched to playing right field and progressed through the playing positions, until once again he became the batter.

Among the boys playing at the 61st Street playground was a neighborhood boy named Danny Wakefield. At the time no one could have guessed that one day he would become a well-known author of several award winning short stories, essays and books, including *Starting Over, New York in the Fifties* and *Going All the Way*. The latter book's story line was set on the north side of Indianapolis during the 1950s. Both of the main characters, Sonny and Gunner, were graduates of the mythical high school "Shortly," which in actuality was Shortridge High School. Also a Shortridge graduate, Dan Wakefield followed in the footsteps of his high school predecessor, author Kurt Vonnegut.

At no time were any adults involved in our sports, either as coaches or spectators. In addition, there was no park staff to make our lives miserable. If a player didn't like a call or there was a difference of opinion among the players, we just worked it out among ourselves. My parents never saw me play any sport while I was in grade school, nor did most of my playmates' parents. There were no Little League teams then, but some of the local churches did have organized youth sports programs such as the C.Y.O. (Catholic Youth Organization) and Tabernacle Presbyterian Church. Some grade schools also had football and baseball teams, but they didn't play during the summer months.

Perhaps the greatest fun of all for us boys and girls was the word in the neighborhood that a circus was coming to town. During the 1930s and 1940s several circuses visited Indianapolis including the Roy Rogers Thrill Circus, the Shrine Circus, the Cole Brothers Circus and most famous of all, the Ringling Brothers, Barnum and Bailey Circus known as the B & B circus. Most important, the circus was the only chance for kids to see real live wild animals because Indianapolis didn't have a zoo. Even more fun than seeing the circus itself was watching the unloading of the animals, tents and paraphernalia when the circus train arrived in town. When the word went out in the neighborhood that the B & B circus was unloading at the nearby State Fairgrounds railroad siding, we boys rode our bikes over to watch the proceedings. At the time transporting the huge circus entourage required the use of four streamlined trains arriving at one hour intervals totaling one hundred double length railroad cars.

The B & B circus newspaper ad in 1940 stated that there would be fifty elephants, eight hundred performers and one hundred clowns. It was fun to watch those trained elephants as they were unloaded from their box cars and in turn the elephants helped unload the tents and equipment. The best part of all was watching the unloading of the big cats housed in portable wagon cages. That year the circus featured an amazing number of different "man eaters" including tigers, leopards, panthers, pumas, cougars, jaguars and lions. We looked forward to seeing them perform in the center ring going through their routine as commanded by lion tamer Frank Buck. Of course we had previously heard about Frank Buck and his wild animals which were featured in his best selling book, *Bring 'Em Back Alive*. We also knew about his one competitor for big cat fame, Clyde Beatty, "Big Game Hunter," who joined forces with the Cole Brothers Circus in the 1930s.

Up to the middle 1950s traveling circus shows were still carried by train and performances were still held in the "Big Top" tent. Even a disastrous 1944 fire in a Hartford, Connecticut, circus tent where over one hundred spectators were killed did not put an end to the outdoor setting. The switch to indoor arenas was simply a matter of economics. It became too expensive for the circus companies to maintain the large crew required to set up and take down the forty tents needed to shelter the entire operation for just a one or two-day performance. It was less costly and more flexible for the circus entourage to travel by truck, bus and automobile trailer than by train.

As we boys reached our middle teens it was great fun to see the sideshows. Our favorite was the freak show where one of the performers such as the sword swallower performed a short act out in front as the sideshow barker tried to entice us inside to see the rest of the show. The inside freak show entourage included the giant "all seven feet of him," the fat lady, and the tattooed man all of which had their loyal fans. Today many of those so-called "freaks" of yesteryear wouldn't get a second look out in public.

Before the 500-mile race in May 1946, Rhude and I rode our bikes out to the Indianapolis Motor Speedway on the first day of qualifications to see what was happening. We had eagerly waited for the postwar reopening of the Speedway for auto racing. The track had remained closed during the war years and had just been purchased by Tony Hulman. Tony, who owned several businesses in Terre Haute, refurbished the track for the 1946 race. As we neared the Motor Speedway on Georgetown Road, we saw some boys perched in tall trees on a farm adjacent to the north end of the track. Apparently the boys had discovered a way to view the track activities for free. The Speedway's seven-foot high wooden fence kept out most of the freeloaders. When we parked our bikes along the fence, we noticed that strips of wood had been nailed to some of the tree trunks for easy access. One of the tree sitters said that the rule was whoever reached the trees first had squatter's rights. Needless to say we rode our bikes out there very early on subsequent race qualification days. As a precautionary measure, we loaded down our bikes with a supply of short wood strips and a hammer and nails. From our high perch, Rhude and I hoped to get a glimpse of car #29 driven by Ted Horn. He was one of our favorite drivers before the War along with Maurie Rose and Rex Mays. As it turned out Ted Horn finished third in the 1946 race. Perhaps the best part of all was that sitting high in the trees we could actually see and hear the cars as they zoomed around the track during qualifications and not just have to read about the cars and drivers in the newspaper. The first live television broadcast of the big race didn't take place until 1949.

Rhude and I often rode our Schwinn bicycles to other distant places such as Riverside Park located about four miles from our homes. Riverside Amusement Park dated back to the late 1800s and by the 1940s it offered the typical rides found in amusement parks of the period ranging from a Ferris wheel to a merry-go-round. Our favorites were the two roller coasters appropriately named the Thriller and the Flash as well as the Fun house and Dodge-Em bumper cars. By 1950 it was estimated that the park's yearly attendance reached 1,000,000 visitors. It certainly didn't hurt attendance that there was no entry fee until years later.

Another favorite place to visit by bike was the nearby Riviera Club. The "Rivy," founded in 1933, was primarily a private swimming club although other sport activities were offered as well. We boys biked there often during the summer months whenever we were not playing baseball, working at a summer job or doing chores around the house. For us the Rivy was more of a social experience than a place to swim. We rarely ventured into the water at the Rivy but sat poolside to talk sports and ogle the girls.

Another Rivy activity was going down into what we called the gold mine to search for hidden treasure. One of the guys had discovered that the entrance to the basement level of the building was below the boys' and girls' changing rooms. The flooring in the first floor dressing rooms was made of wide, rough wooden slats, which had about a one-inch gap between the boards. Apparently in the process of dressing or undressing, a lot of kids dropped loose change through the floorboards to the lower level. I must admit that I was too scared to go down there to search for treasure, but I heard many stories about how much money some kids found in the gold mine.

All too often I arrived home from the Rivy with a bright red sunburn which hopefully would turn into a deep tan. Sunscreen lotions had not been invented. Even if they were available, no self-respecting boy would have used them. Skin lotions of any type were strictly for girls. If a boy was seen using any lotion, he would have been called a sissy or a mama's boy. We felt it was better to act like a he-man (as we defined the term) and suffer the consequences. Common sense, reason, and logic took a back seat then and perhaps still do today.

Besides the bicycle another popular kid vehicle was the pushmobile. Although most of us boys didn't compete in pushmobile races, we did enjoy constructing and driving such vehicles around the neighborhood. As soon as we had constructed the car out of old orange crates, scrap wood, miscellaneous hardware, steering ropes and pulleys and wheels off an old wagon or baby carriage, we needed to find a pusher. In those days a pusher was another boy willing to push the racer rather than ride in and steer it. Pushing was done with an old broomstick placed in a small notch drilled in the center of the rear bumper. There were endless arguments about who should be the driver and who should be the pusher. This argument was eliminated for some enterprising boys who managed to hook up an old Briggs and Stratton motor salvaged from a derelict washing machine to the rear axle of the pushmobile, converting it into a self-propelled racecar.

The popularity of the pushmobile in Indianapolis can be traced back to June 1912 when a group of west side boys organized the first local pushmobile race. The fact that the first two Indianapolis 500 mile races had been held at the nearby Speedway track no doubt had an influence on the location of the first pushmobile race. By the early 1930s pushmobile races had become so popular that the city held championship races at the Indianapolis Motor Speedway track as part of the Indy 500 pre-race activities. In 1933, thirty-five boys competed on a three-quarter mile stretch of the track for the opportunity as the winner to drink the coveted glass of milk. About that time someone got the bright idea of letting gravity "push the race cars down a steep hill rather then requiring a pusher on a flat surface. From those early pushmobile races their popularity spread until the races became formalized in the International Soap Box Derby held annually in Akron, Ohio since 1934.

INDIANAPOLIS MOTOR SPEEDWAY PUSHMOBILE
RACE–1933

In Indianapolis a permanent hillside setting for the annual Soap
Box Derby races was constructed near the former Riverside Amusement Park on 30th Street and Cold Spring Road in 1953. It is known
locally as the Wilbur Shaw Memorial Soap Box Derby Hill. Wilbur
Shaw, a three time winner of the Indianapolis 500 mile race, had constructed push mobiles as a youngster and later went on to build and
race dirt track cars before racing at Indy in the big cars.

Many teen-age boys felt they were too old to ride bicycles but
they weren't old enough for beginner's automobile driving permits.
The perfect in-between vehicle was the motor scooter. The status of
owning a motor scooter was indescribable. The owners were the envy
of all the boys who only had bicycles. The only scooter that mattered
to us kids was the Cushman. The Cushman Company even had one
model called the Airborne. Its military counterpart had been an es-
sential piece of equipment used by American paratroopers during
World War II. Being seen on an Airborne motor scooter was about
as he-man as a young teenager could get. For those who didn't want
to be seen riding a bicycle and couldn't afford a motor scooter, there

was still one alternative, the Whizzer motor bike. Initially in 1939 the Whizzer consisted of any standard bicycle mounted with a Whizzer 1 3/8 horsepower engine. In later years the company manufactured their own Whizzer bicycle featuring a Schwinn bike chassis. The bottom line was that most of us couldn't afford the cost of a Whizzer, much less a Cushman, and the Whizzer seemed like not much more than a glorified bicycle.

TRAINS ON THE BRAIN

It all started when I was quite young and received a small wind-up toy train from Santa. The train set consisted of a tin plate locomotive, a coal tender, three passenger cars, ten pieces of two-rail track, and of course a key to wind up the engine. There was just enough track to make a small circle around the Christmas tree. However, it wasn't long before the windup set became boring. Basically all I could do was wind up the locomotive, connect it to the cars on the track, and watch it pull the cars round and round until my eyes glazed over. There had to be something more exciting and there was. My friend Rhude had an extensive electric train layout in his basement which stirred my imagination and I got hooked. It wasn't long before I received a similar O gauge Lionel electric train set for Christmas. No other make such as American Flyer or Marx would do.

My Lionel set consisted of a locomotive, tender, four freight cars, several pieces of three-rail track, and a transformer to power the engine. It wasn't long before my bedroom floor was covered with a more extensive train layout. I saved every nickel and dime to purchase something for my ever expanding train layout. There were so many choices. There were several different types of special use freight cars such as the crane car, automatic dump car and the automated refrigerator milk car and stand. There were neat accessories such as the coal loading station and the log loader. In addition, no train layout was complete without a miniature train station, people and automobiles, not to mention a nearby town with tiny houses and shops. Before long my bedroom floor was crowded with train paraphernalia of every description. When I entered my bedroom I had to be careful where

I walked or it could be like one of those Japanese horror movies in which the monster Godzilla flattened everything in his path.

It wasn't long before much smaller sized train sets came into vogue, perhaps because houses were being constructed with smaller rooms. Consequently, I sold my Lionel train set to one of the younger kids in the neighborhood and replaced it with an HO gauge train layout. The HO cars were about one-third the size of their O gauge counterparts. Once again I started to expand my train layout. One of the fun things about adding to HO gauge train sets was that individual cars could be purchased in kit form. Although I wasn't too skilled in that art form, not having had much luck at piecing together model airplane kits in the past, I was able to assemble a fairly decent looking box car.

As time went on Rhude and I became interested in the real thing. Fortunately Rhude lived just a couple of blocks from the Monon railroad track, and it became our favorite summer playground. The Monon Railroad had its start in 1865 as the Indianapolis, Delphi and Chicago Railway. After several name changes and reorganizations, in 1956 it formally adopted its long-time nickname, the Monon. By the middle 1980's, the Seaboard System, the last owner of the track right of-way, abandoned the line and removed the rails. It is now part of the Indianapolis Greenways System.

Rhude and I spent many happy hours playing along the Monon track between 52nd and 59th Streets. We often competed to see how far we could walk on a rail without losing our balance. If all went well we also jumped rail to rail to see if we could safely land on the other one without falling off. I attributed my track walking skill to inheriting Dad's sure foot on the rail. I have a photo of him walking the rails during a break from his cross-country motor trip from Chicago to Los Angeles in 1923.

DAD RAIL WALKING OUT WEST-1923

Rhude and I enjoyed watching the freight trains and we knew the nicknames of all the different types of freight cars, from the reefer (boxcar refrigerated with large blocks of ice) to the crummy (caboose). We often placed a penny on one rail just before the train's arrival. If it worked, we ended up with a very long and thin penny. We also put one

ear to the rail and waited patiently to hear the sound of an approaching train heading around the bend in the tracks. We had seen this
done by the noble red man in countless Saturday matinee westerns at
the Uptown Theater. With the frequent schedule of both passenger
and freight trains it wasn't long before the rail started humming. I always wondered if one Indian tribe was named the Flatheads because
those unfortunate noble savages often waited a bit too long before
lifting their ears from the rail as the great iron horse approached.

Another fun pastime was playing near Bacon Swamp which ad-
joined the Monon track. From the high ground near the tracks, we
first threw an empty glass bottle as far as possible out into the marshy
area of Bacon Swamp. Borrowing the rocks that the Monon Railroad
Company dumped along the track for ballast, we took turns seeing
who could break the bottle with an accurate throw. Earlier we tried
using a homemade slingshot cut from a forked tree branch and bound
with thin strips of old rubber inner tubes to propel the missile. Unfortunately the slingshot was not very accurate. As we grew older we
took our BB guns to the swamp to break empty glass bottles floating
on the muddy waters. At that time, Bacon Swamp was still a wet peat
bog covering most of the area bordered by Keystone Avenue on the
east, the Monon tracks on the west, Kessler Boulevard (59th street) on
the north and 54th Street on the south. In the summer we never went
near the water's edge. Rumor had it that the swamp was filled with
water moccasins and that there was quicksand lurking just beneath
the surface of the pond. However, in the winter we walked out on the
frozen ice to see how far we could venture without cracking it. By the
1950s the swamp was partially filled in to make way for a housing
development and later a retirement community. A small portion of
the original swamp is still there and called Bacon Lake, adjoining the
American Village retirement complex.

As we reached our teens and became more mobile, we boys rode
our bikes down to the Boulevard Station, also known as the Maple
Road Station on 38th Street adjacent to the State Fairgrounds. The
Monon station had been constructed in 1922 to serve north side
passenger trains. We became friends with the stationmaster Martin
Benefiel, affectionately known as Benny. In time we were introduced
to the diesel freight engineers who stopped at the 38th street station

on their way back to the 22ⁿᵈ Street roundhouse. It wasn't long before we were allowed to ride in the cab with the engineers to the round-house. From there we were happy to walk the tracks sixteen blocks back to our bikes at the Boulevard Station.

My first contact with the 38th Street station was in the 1930s, when our family took infrequent overnight trips to Chicago. We boarded the sleeping car at the Boulevard Station at about 10:00 PM and bed-ded down in the berths for the night. A short time later the Chicago Limited coming from downtown Indianapolis Union Station made a brief stop at the 38th Street station to hook up our sleeping car. We arrived in Chicago early the next morning, refreshed after a good night's rest. Rail travel was still popular when I had my first train ride. At that time 167 passenger trains entered and left Indianapolis Union Station every twenty-four hours.

MONON BOULEVARD RAILROAD STATION-1930S

STREETCAR, BUS OR TROLLEY

In our neighborhood few businessmen drove downtown since they lived near the extensive public transportation system of streetcar, bus or trackless trolley lines. In 1937 Indianapolis Railway officials estimated that ninety five percent of the population lived within three blocks of public transportation. Street railway service was inaugurated in Indianapolis during the Civil War. The first trolley line, cars drawn by mules, extended from the downtown Union Station to nearby Military Park, which at the time was the State Fairgrounds. By 1894, a line was constructed to Broad Ripple village when the entire system was converted from mule drawn cars to electric vehicles. The trackless trolley was introduced to Indianapolis in 1932 with the purchase of fifteen vehicles. Like the streetcar, the trackless trolley received its power from a series of overhead wires through the trolley pantograph. The trackless trolleys were fast, quiet and did not pollute the air like diesel buses. On the north side of town, in addition to the College streetcar lane, a bus line ran along Central Avenue one block west of our house, and a trackless trolley line ran a few blocks away along Pennsylvania Street, terminating on the north side at 52nd Street.

Dad enjoyed riding the nearby College Avenue streetcar line downtown to work. The ride was inexpensive, convenient, and gave him thirty minutes each way to engage in his favorite pastime which was reading. The streetcar dropped him off in downtown Indianapolis, a few blocks from his Westinghouse office on south Pennsylvania Street. That office building was razed in 1998 and replaced by the Conseco Fieldhouse which became the new home of the Pacers' basketball team. The number of daily streetcar trips made by my father was greater in the 1930s, when the typical office workweek was six days, with only Sunday as a day of rest. In later years Dad worked only Saturday mornings on the weekends, and finally by the 1950s he enjoyed just a five-day workweek.

As with other streetcar lines in Indianapolis in the 1920s and 1930s, retail shopping and professional offices were built along the line that ran north on College Avenue to 63rd Street and then east on Broad Ripple Avenue. I also remember the interurban car in the late 1930s that ran along College Avenue on the streetcar track and terminated its run in Kokomo, IN. The interurban car was to outlying regions what the streetcar, bus, and trackless trolley were to the city. Interurban stops were made on the north side of Indianapolis at the State School for the Blind near Broad Ripple and at Home Place. The line carried both passengers and freight, including livestock and other animals. Unfortunately by 1940 the interurban system was out of business in Indiana. The first Indianapolis traction terminal power substation still stands at the corner of College Avenue and 64th Street in Broad Ripple. In later years it became the home of American Legion Post #312.

The College streetcar line was convenient to our doctor's office, the Uptown Movie Theater and a post office sub-station, all of which were located at 42nd and College Avenue. Also, the one smaller north side department store, Nick Kerz, was a short streetcar ride away at 34th and College Avenue. The College streetcar line was originally designed to terminate on the north side at the Broad Ripple amusement park, a few blocks east of 63rd and College Avenue along White River.

For those more expensive or hard-to-find items, the family rode the streetcar downtown to shop at one of the three major department stores: Wm. H. Blocks, L.S. Ayres, or H.P. Wassons. I can still remember walking through those strange department store revolving doors and being thrust into a surreal world of sophisticated looking lady clerks, exotic smells and the sound of soft music floating through the air. It seemed as if the whole first floor of the department store was filled with dazzling display cases crammed with every imaginable type of powder, mascara, perfume and jewelry. I felt as if I had stumbled onto a movie set and expected to see Myrna Loy, Joan Crawford or Barbara Stanwyck make an appearance at any minute. As a child I felt very intimidated by the experience and was happy when we finally made our way back to the escalators. I never did find out who purchased all of those expensive cosmetics— it certainly wasn't my Mom or any of her friends.

Another unusual downtown sight came with the March of Dimes Crusade held each spring by the National Foundation for Infantile Paralysis. The drive raised research funds to aid children who were the most susceptible to Infantile Paralysis, more commonly called polio. A polio epidemic struck Indiana about every ten years starting in 1916 when six thousand children, most of them under the age of five, died in the U.S. Indianapolis had its own severe outbreaks of polio in 1940 and 1949.

To raise funds for research, dimes were solicited by volunteers stationed outside the entrance to L.S. Ayres on Washington Street. As dimes were donated they were placed down on the broad expanse of sidewalk next to the thousands of dimes already collected. The annual event was appropriately called the Mile of Dimes. By the end of the drive, the sidewalk looked liked a shiny, wide, silver carpet stretching as far as the eye could see. As a child I wondered what happened to those dimes when the sun went down. Did they have to be picked up every night and repositioned on the sidewalk every morning, or perhaps a dime guard was hired to patrol the area after dark.

What was also poignant about polio was that it laid waste to adults as well as children. One adult victim was President Franklin Delano Roosevelt. At the age of thirty nine years, Roosevelt contracted polio after a boating accident near his summer home on Campobello Island, near New Brunswick, Canada. For many years, the general public didn't know that the president had been paralyzed from the waist down since 1921. Roosevelt went to great lengths to hide his disability, as he was afraid that his political career would be over if his disability was discovered. (He was permanently bound to a wheelchair.) Although later newsreel footage showed him apparently walking short distances, in actuality he was dragging his legs along, weighed down by ten pounds of steel leg supports. An aide or family member always supported one of his arms. It is to the credit of the press at the time that his secret disability was not disclosed until after his death in 1945.

Another reason to go downtown was to shop at Stout's shoe store, which is still in business today at the same location on Massachusetts Avenue. Mary Ellen and I could hardly wait to place our feet in the fluoroscope machine. When the switch was turned on, you could actually see the bones in your foot glowing green in the dark. After a pair of shoes was selected, the clerk put the payment and shoes back in the box and placed it in a wire basket which hung from an overhead wire. The clerk pulled on a long rope cord which sent the basket on an overhead trolley system whizzing to a second floor office. There the shoes were wrapped and the payment transaction finalized. The parcel was then placed in the basket and sent back by the same overhead wire system to the waiting clerk on the first floor. For a kid it was a fun thing to watch.

As a young teenager I was finally considered old enough to ride downtown on the College Avenue streetcar without my Mom. The destination for us schoolboy chums was usually a penny arcade in the 200 block of North Illinois Street. That section of Illinois Street in the 1930s and 1940s was rather tawdry. Once in a while we walked by the Fox Burlesque Theater and looked at the large posters that illustrated coming attractions, usually strip tease shows. It was several more years before we were old enough to venture inside to see the likes of Rose La Rose and hear the off-color jokes of the comedian Scurvy. Along that section of Illinois Street were also package liquor stores, smoke shops, second rate movie theaters such as the Alamo, fleabag flophouses, greasy spoon lunchrooms, and worst of all a tattoo parlor. In those days only men got tattoos, and they were typically either drunken sailors or men who viewed living in a derelict house trailer down by White River as a step up in life.

My first experience seeing someone with a real tattoo was when I was in basic training in the U.S. Army. However, when I was only eight, for some reason I wanted a tattoo of my own. Maybe it was because my favorite cartoon character Popeye had an anchor tattooed on each of his massive forearms. One day I spied a packet of simulated tattoos for sale at Danner Brothers store in Broad Ripple. At least the packet said that they were tattoos. For 10 cents I purchased 22 different designs featuring ships, subs, planes, and Don Winslow's fighting Navy pals. Don Winslow, an officer in the Navy, was a popular comic strip character during World War II. As soon as I reached home, I filled a pan with water, soaked one of the transfer tattoos until it was ready, and then had the really big decision to make. Where was I going to put that tattoo? I finally decided to put it on one of my skinny forearms and I spent the rest of the day flashing the tattoo to anyone coming my way.

Another fun downtown activity was a visit to the joke and novelty shop located just off Monument Circle on West Market Street next to the old English Theater building. It was the perfect place to purchase cigarette loads, itching powder, whoopee cushions, dribble glasses, and plastic ice cubes which supposedly had real insects trapped inside. For hard to find items, we boys browsed through the mail order Johnson Smith novelty catalog. One of their most popular items was the car bomb, which was to be wired to an auto spark plug. When the unsuspecting driver turned the ignition on, the bomb emitted a shrill whistle followed by a very loud noise and a huge cloud of dense black smoke. We boys never purchased the bombs, since none of us was old enough to own a car, and we were afraid to try the experiment on someone else's automobile.

On rare occasions as an older teenager I took the trackless trolley home after a late night sojourn downtown since the streetcars stopped running around midnight. I won't forget riding the trackless trolley late one evening. After an uneventful ride, the driver was not paying attention and didn't stop in time to make the end of the line turn-around at 52nd and Pennsylvania Streets. The trolley's dual pantograph went off the overhead wires and we coasted almost to 53rd street before the trolley came to a halt. I didn't mind it, because I was then one block closer to home.

The College Avenue streetcar line was abandoned in 1955, as was the trackless trolley system in 1959. In the 1960s a small one-story ranch house was constructed at the site of the former trackless trolley turnaround at 52nd and Pennsylvania Streets. Unfortunately the "turn-a-round" house doesn't match the scale or architectural style of the other houses in the Meridian-Kessler neighborhood, most of which were built in the 1920s.

AUTOMOBILE TRIPS

My first dim recollection of taking a long automobile ride was in the summer of 1934 when the family drove to the Chicago World's Fair from Indianapolis. The Fair, also known as the Century of Progress Exposition, commemorated the one hundredth anniversary of the founding of Chicago. The fair was constructed on 427 acres along Lake Michigan, much of which was landfill. Although it was during the heart of the Depression and extra money was scarce, Dad had two reasons for wanting to go. First of all it had been some time since he had visited his parents and brothers and families, all of whom lived in the Chicago area. More importantly, Chicago fairs had a special meaning for him. Dad was born in Chicago in May 1893, coincidentally at the start of the great World's Columbian Exposition held in Chicago that same year.

The 1893 Exposition observed the four hundredth anniversary of Christopher Columbus' arrival in America and was perhaps the greatest World's Fair ever. The fair covered 666 acres and had many innovative architectural features and firsts. For example, the building housing the manufacturing and liberal arts exhibits was the largest one ever constructed up to that time anywhere in the world, spanning nearly forty acres alone. Many products we use today were introduced during the six-month run of the fair, including Cracker Jack, Shredded Wheat, Juicy Fruit gum, Aunt Jemima pancake mix, and Pabst Blue Ribbon beer.

The crowning achievement of the 1893 Exposition was the erection of the first Ferris wheel. This gargantuan ride towered 240 feet into the sky with thirty-six cars, each of which could hold fifty people. During the fair run the one-day attendance soared to over three hundred thousand people, the largest one-day attendance of any entertainment venue ever. Over one hundred years later, only the Palace of Fine Arts, now known as the Chicago Museum of Science and Industry, remains as a testimonial to that unsurpassed extravaganza.

In honor of the event, the United States Mint produced a special Columbian commemorative half-dollar in 1893. Dad was given one of the coins as a young boy by his father and was told wonderful stories about the 1893 Exposition. Dad proudly carried that half-dollar in his trouser pocket for the rest of his life. With those connections to fairs in Chicago there was no stopping him from going to the 1934 Chicago World's Fair.

My only recollection of visiting the fair at the tender age of three was of a somewhat scary experience. I remember walking with my family along the crowded walkways and being mesmerized by all of the strange sights and sounds. We stopped in front of a funny little house with strange doors. When the doors opened I followed my family inside a small room as did several other people. All of a sudden the doors clanged shut; a man pushed a lever, and I felt a strange sensation of the room moving. Dad reassured me that everything was fine and not to worry. We left that room after a short ride and were

ushered into another small room with windows. Then that room began to move as well, only instead of going up it went sideways. At
the time I didn't understand that I had taken my first elevator ride to
the top of what was known as the Sky Ride and then walked into an
overhead cable car shaped like a rocket. Supported by overhead wires,
the car traveled back and forth some eighteen hundred feet to another
tall tower located in the middle of the fairgrounds. This popular attraction gave passengers a bird's eye view of the fair from two hundred
feet in the air.

However, the most popular attraction by far at the World's Fair
and the one that was still talked about years later was exotic dancer
Sally Rand. She was featured in the Streets of Paris concession on
the Midway. Sally, wearing little but a big smile, put on a daring strip
tease act. Her only props were two large ostrich feather fans that she
manipulated like a pro. Sally's show was so successful financially that
many credited her with saving the Chicago Worlds Fair from possible
bankruptcy.

SALLY RAND AND HER FANS

During our day at the Chicago World's Fair, Dad planned to take in some of the more technical exhibits. Stating that the rest of the family would find them boring, he suggested that we split up and meet in a couple of hours at a designated place. When we met later, Dad said he really enjoyed the technical exhibits. In looking back at that Chicago Fair adventure many years later, I wondered if Dad thought that Sally Rand fell into the category of a technical exhibit.

The 1933 Chicago World's Fair was just the beginning for Sally Rand's long stage career. She was still plying her trade at the age of sixty-four when she appeared in June 1969 at the Town & Country Lounge in Indianapolis. When asked how she could continue to perform her strip tease act of three to five shows a day at such an advanced age, she replied, "You just try to take care of the equipment" and "What in heaven's name is strange about a grandmother dancing nude? I'll bet lots of grandmothers do it."

In the ensuing years, every summer our family drove to the extended family summer place on Brown's Lake in southern Wisconsin for our annual two-week vacation. We used U.S. Route 52 and then Route 41 to Chicago for the mandatory overnight stay with our cousins in Villa Park, Illinois and then on to the south side of Chicago to have a brief visit with my Mom's sister Louise and their elderly mother, Grandma Bodevin. They lived in an apartment on the south side of Chicago near 67th and Stony Island Street. Their apartment was one of our favorite places to visit. First of all it was our only chance to see the inside of an apartment building because in Indianapolis we didn't know anybody who lived in one. During our visit we kids rode the four-floor elevator up and down over and over again. More importantly the visit gave us a chance to see and talk to the landlady's parrot. As soon as we said hello to Grandma and Aunt Louise, we raced down the hall and knocked on the landlady's door, in hopes of some parrot talk. When things got boring in the apartment our parents took pity on us and let us play on the swings just across the street in Jackson Park.

While visiting my Mom's family we loved to have lunch in downtown Chicago at the Marshall Field & Co. department store. Marshall Fields was to Chicago what Blocks and Ayres were to Indianapolis, although Fields was much larger and more elegant. Eating lunch there was similar to dining at the local L.S. Ayres Tea Room only fancier. The best part of having lunch at Fields was getting there. Since my grandmother and aunt never learned to drive we knew that a ride downtown on the elevated train called the "El" was in store. We had to walk just a few blocks from the apartment building to the "EL" stop near 63rd and Stony Island. To Mary Ellen and me the ride was almost as much fun as Riverside Amusement Park in Indy.

The elevated train ride had the feel of a combination roller coaster and bumper car as it swung and swayed around curves on its way downtown. Once on the train, we made sure to get window seats so that we could look down and see what went on in people's backyards. It was amazing to us what people stored there, from junk cars to old iron bedsteads and refrigerators. Those were certainly neat things that would have been impossible to see from a street view of the houses and apartment buildings.

Once we arrived at the Field's restaurant and were seated by the hostess, we were given the very extensive lunch menu to browse. My grandmother very graciously said for us to order anything we liked on the menu as the treat was on her. Mary Ellen usually selected something fancy that was never served at home such as a crab salad. Having been there before on previous annual trips I knew exactly what I wanted which was a peanut butter and jelly sandwich and a glass of chocolate milk. When it came to food my working philosophy was always to stay with the tried and true. Why take a chance on eating something new that just might not be very good? After lunch and a quick tour of the Marshall Fields department store we once again had the fun of riding the elevated train back to 63rd Street and Stony Island.

Then on to Wisconsin. During the drive we passed through many farm areas where we spotted the small red and white Burma Shave signs which first appeared in 1927. Over the years, we memorized many of the jingles. My favorites were "Don't pass cars on curve or hill; if the cops don't get you the morticians will" and "Hardly a driver is now alive who passed on hills at 75."

The other familiar ad of the day was painted on the sides of barns in three-foot-high letters: "Chew Mail Pouch Tobacco–Treat Yourself to the Best." The Mail Pouch Tobacco barn advertisement traces its history back a little over 100 years when the Bloch brothers of Wheeling, West Virginia, started selling the first chewing tobacco, *West Virginia Mail Pouch*, which they later shortened to Mail Pouch. Soon after the turn of the century, the brothers decided to embark on a marketing campaign and selected rural barns as the place to get their message across to their most likely customers. Those customers were men who worked in coal mines, saw mills, grain elevators or around other flammable products and consequently were not allowed to smoke on the job.

Over the years some thirty thousand barns were painted with the familiar slogan: "Chew Mail Pouch Tobacco–Treat Yourself to the Best." The greatest concentration of barn signs was in rural areas in the east and midwest. Painting teams scoured the countryside, looking for farmers willing to have the ad painted on their barns. As an added inducement, the farmers were often paid a few dollars compensation in addition to a free paint job. The most famous Mail Pouch barn painter was Harley Warrick who worked for the Bloch brothers for fifty years. During that time Harley painted ten thousand barns many of which were repaints. The beginning of the end for Mail Pouch barn signs came when the Federal Highway Beautification Act was enacted in 1975, with the prodding of Ladybird Johnson. Harley was the sole barn painter for Bloch Brothers for the next twenty-five years, until his death in 2000, during which time he was interviewed many times for national radio and television broadcasts.

HARLEY WARRICK PAINTING A
MAIL POUCH TOBACCO BARN

The journey to Brown's Lake in southern Wisconsin from Indianapolis took about six hours in our 1933 Buick, whereas today with the modern interstates it takes about four and one-half hours. The trip was not complete without stopping at the Nu-Joy restaurant in Kentland, Indiana, for a double dip ice cream cone. We considered ourselves fortunate if we didn't have to stop for an overheated radiator or to change a flat tire. In those days we carried a tire pump, inner tube repair kit, and a spare tire or two for insurance.

Once we arrived at the family's summer cottage, our days were filled with croquet, horseshoes, boating, fun in the water, and the two-mile walk into the town of Burlington for a chocolate soda at Reinhardie's Drug Store. Our stay at the cottage was a step back in time. There was no running water, so we took turns with the hand pump behind the house, and our icebox sat on the back porch waiting for the arrival of the iceman every other day. The outhouse was located a discrete distance from the cottage.

One stroke of luck was that our lake property was just a couple of lots away from Moore's Lakeside Resort. Many wealthy Chicago families spent vacations there every summer. Among the many attractions Moore's offered was live evening entertainment every weekend. Comedians, singers and other entertainers were brought in from nearby Chicago and other Midwestern locations. Every weekend evening as young teenagers my cousins, Mary Ellen, and I walked along the shoreline to the resort where we mingled with the resort guests to see and hear the entertainment for free.

Back in Indianapolis during the summer, we went on Sunday picnics to one of our favorite locations called Woollen's Garden. It was a little-used fifty-five acre city park and nature preserve along Fall Creek, just west of Shadeland Avenue. The park's main attraction was its peaceful forest setting along the creek with many birds and native plants. Unlike the other nearby parks we visited, there were nature trails to walk. Unfortunately in more recent times Woollen's Garden has become land locked with the construction of Interstate 465 just east of the park and an apartment complex to the south.

We also journeyed to Northern Beach, a small private park operated by our former Carrollton Avenue neighbors the Schmuttes. The park is located in the town of Carmel on 116th Street near White

River. In the 1930s and 1940s, after paying a small entry fee to their son Carl at the gate, we could use all of the facilities including picnic tables, a large swimming pool, horseshoe pits, badminton courts, and playground equipment. Several years ago the park was acquired by the neighboring Oak Hill Mansion organization. Now the park is private, caters only to large groups (a minimum of sixty people), and does not allow any food to be brought in.

The most popular park for our family picnics was Forest Park in Noblesville. Quite new when we first used it, this one hundred and eighty-acre park was constructed by the WPA during the Depression. When we were smaller children, our favorite activities were swinging on the giant swings, sliding down the circular slide, riding on the large teeter-totters and playing miniature golf. We seldom took advantage of the large swimming pool that is still in use today. Of course no picnic was complete without Mom's fried chicken, potato salad, Boston baked beans, hot cloverleaf rolls, sweet pickles and deviled eggs, chocolate cake for desert, and homemade lemonade. For variety, once in a while Mom substituted hot dogs and hamburgers for the chicken. The meat was grilled on one of the many fire pits and barbecue grills scattered throughout the park. Many years later I spent a great deal of time in Forest Park at the Indiana Transportation Museum volunteering with the first Fair Train, which had its maiden trip in 1983 from Noblesville to the Indiana State Fairgrounds over the old Monon tracks.

From time to time our family journeyed by car to some of Indiana's state parks. Our favorites were McCormick's Creek and Turkey Run. Although walking through the woods on rugged trails was fun, the best part was climbing up the steps to the top of one of the CCC (Civilian Construction Corps) fire towers to get a true bird's eye view of the surrounding scenery. The towers ranged in height from about one hundred to one hundred and fifty feet. Unfortunately many of them fell into disuse years ago, due to technological advances in forest fire spotting, and most of the towers were subsequently razed.

Kindergarten And Elementary School

Unfortunately life for us kids was not all about trips, holidays, and summer fun. I still remember my Mom and Dad saying that if I ever wanted to amount to anything I had to go to school. Their thoughts were later reinforced by a saying I had to memorize in grade school: "A little learning is a dangerous thing; drink deep, or taste not the Pierian spring."

My academic journey started in 1936 when I attended the Broad Ripple Free Kindergarten. It was housed in a one-story building which is adjacent to the Vogue Theater on College Avenue. My major recollections of kindergarten include spending an inordinate amount of time napping on a small wool rug, making unidentifiable objects out of clay, drawing unidentifiable objects with crayons and helping tend a small flower and vegetable garden in the back yard of the building. A special treat for us boys and girls was a field trip to the Broad Ripple Amusement Park, adjacent to White River along Broad Ripple Avenue. By 1936 the park still had many thrill rides including a roller coaster and Ferris wheel, as well as many kiddy rides such as a carousel. My favorite, the carousel, was later moved to the Indianapolis Children's Museum and is now listed on the National Register of Historic Places.

In 1937 my parents decided to purchase a larger home at 54th and Park Avenue, a few blocks away from our former Carrollton Avenue rental house. The new home had one additional bedroom so that my sister and I could have some privacy. At the new house, Mary Ellen and I were still able to attend Public School 84, located at 57th Street and Central Avenue. The school was also known as the Joseph Bingham Elementary School. Joseph Bingham, born in New York City in 1815, was elected to the first Indianapolis School Board in 1871 and served for eleven years. Seventy-eight years after it was erected, PS 84 is still open and is now home to kindergarten through eighth grade students.

In the 1930s and 1940s children living in about a one-mile radius of the school attended PS 84 in the first through eighth grades. The area served by the school extended from 53rd Street on the south, the Broad Ripple Canal on the north, Winthrop St. on the east and Meridian St. on the west, and also included an area "out in the country" north of the Broad Ripple canal and the community of Crow's Nest near the White River. Most kids walked several blocks to school, although older kids were allowed to ride their bikes. Some pampered boys and girls were driven to school by a parent. The school was very democratic in that its boundaries encompassed students from the big mansions along Meridian Street and Crow's Nest on the west side to small rental bungalows on the east side adjacent to the Monon railroad tracks. A few of the wealthier neighborhood kids went to the private Park School for boys or the Tudor Hall School for girls. However, other wealthy kids opted for our public school.

Such was the case with Bob Baxter, a classmate I played with who lived in a large house in the 5600 block of north Pennsylvania Street. I didn't pay much attention to the house itself although it had a two and one half story vaulted living room ceiling and a real pine paneled basement recreation room. That room had a ping-pong table which, when not in use, was covered with an amazing variety of seashells from the family's winter Florida vacations. What really impressed me was my chance to eat real ice cream whenever I went to Bob's for a visit. At home, we only had ice cream with our Sunday dinner, and it was usually homemade, bearing little resemblance to the real thing. I thought that always having store-bought ice cream in the refrigerator to eat at any time was a sign of real wealth.

Another classmate, Sue Goodman, lived in a large mansion in Crow's Nest off Kessler Boulevard. Again, I was not impressed with the fifteen-room house and the five-car garage, or with being chauffeured in her parents' limousine to nearby Schoener's Drugstore at 56th and Illinois Street. What really impressed me was when Sue treated me to a chocolate soda. As we left the drug store after enjoying the sodas, Sue walked out without paying. I said to her, "Did you forget to pay?" She replied, "I don't need to, my family has a charge account here." I had never heard of a charge account. I thought, "Boy, her parents must be somebody special."

Catholic children in the neighborhood went to St. Joan of Arc Elementary School at 42nd and Park Avenue, next to the Catholic Church. The Jewish children in our neighborhood attended PS 84 and after school were bussed to the Kirshbaum Center at 2300 N. Meridian Street for additional schooling. Their studies included the Torah and other Old Testament scriptures, as well as the Hebrew language, and Jewish history.

In those days Christianity was part of the classroom experience in public school. At the start of the school day we gave the pledge of allegiance to the flag, followed by a Christian prayer. We were required to memorize bible passages from both the Old and New Testaments. I can still remember in grade school learning the 23rd Psalm, King James Version of course. We sang religious Christmas carols and hymns such as Onward Christian Soldiers. Religious songs were included in *The Gray Book of Favorite Songs* used by the Indianapolis Public School system at the time. We also memorized patriotic poems and parts of historical documents and speeches such as the Preamble to the U.S. Constitution and some of Lincoln's Gettysburg Address.

Outside of the classroom we memorized a lot of nonsensical poems such as the following which unfortunately I still remember after sixty-five years. "Standing on the corner; not doing any harm. Along comes a cop and grabs me by the arm. Drags me round the corner and rings a funny bell. Along comes a paddy wagon and takes me to a cell. Next morning when I awake, I look upon the wall. The roaches and the bedbugs are having a game of ball. The score is one to nothing and the roaches are ahead. A bedbug hits a homer and knocks me out of bed."

As we moved into our middle teen years we memorized more ribald poems and sayings that were certainly not part of the school curriculum. Typical sayings were passed on by word of mouth such as: "Confucius say, 'She was only the farmer's daughter, but all of the horse men-knew-her.'" A typical rhyming couplet: "There was a young woman from Cape Cod, who thought that all creatures came from God, but it wasn't the Almighty who lifted her nightie, it was Roger the lodger by God." Fictitious book titles we passed along included *The Golden Stream* by I. P. Daily and *The Chinese Mystery* by Who Flung Dung.

Back in the classroom at PS 84, we were blessed with the frequent appearance of Mrs. Emma Grayce Peed. She was employed by the Indianapolis school system to teach penmanship to younger students at several area grade schools. Mrs. Peed was tall, older, dignified, and no-nonsense like most of our schoolteachers. On her first visit of the school term, she handed out her own thirty-two page writing manual entitled *The Write-Well Handwriting Manual.* Each of the pages constituted a weekly lesson plan for handwriting practice. The top half of the page had illustrations of the proper way to write various words. The lower half of the page was left blank for students to try to copy the top half handwriting. We handed in our booklets each week to be graded. Before tackling the more difficult aspects of cursive writing, we were required to make endless circles, which were profusely illustrated in the writing manual. To make those circles, we first had to check that our stick pen had the necessary supply of ink in reserve. I can still remember her saying "Make those circles—round and round—make those circles." I am not sure how well we did with other letters of the alphabet, but boy we sure could write some swell looking O's.

Mrs. Peed and her family lived in an old farmhouse just one block north of School 84 at the corner of Central Avenue and 58th Street. All of Mrs. Peed's sons were quite talented. The oldest, Bill, became the senior cartoonist for Walt Disney Productions in its early years. One of Bill's earliest art assignments was on the film *Fantasia*, released in 1940, which has become a cartoon classic. Later Bill Peet, as he called himself, became a nationally recognized author of children's books, of which he wrote some thirty five in all. In addition to writing the stories, he drew all of the illustrations. I imagine that he changed his last name from Peed to Peet because it sounded more dignified. We certainly kidded our classmate Jim, his younger brother, about his last name. Jim became a nationally recognized furniture designer. A long article about his life appeared in the January 9, 1995 edition of the *Indianapolis Star.* A third son, George, is best known for his character designs used in the early 1960's animated cartoon series entitled *The Mighty Hercules.*

A few of us boys dreaded the arrival of the report cards we received three times a semester. It wasn't so much the grades that were a worry, since most of us did all right in the scholastic field. It was in deportment, also known as citizenship, where some of us had a problem. We were graded on such important personal traits as industry, dependability, cooperation, and courtesy. The 1-2-3 point grading system was in vogue, with 1 being the best mark. I was often marked down for "talks too much" or "needs improvement in Works Steadily." As an added inducement to do well, there was an explicit threat on the report card in capital letters, stating that "repetition of the figure 3 indicates another semester in the grade may be necessary."

SCHOOL FASHIONS AND FADS

Starting with the very first grade, we boys adhered to an informal dress code as follows: first and second grade boys wore short pants; third and fourth graders wore knickers and knee stockings, and fifth through eighth graders wore long pants. None of the boys wore overalls; they were considered too informal for school wear. Even in those days, kids in grade school were slaves to fashion and creatures of habit. One of those creatures of our habit was the infamous raccoon skin cap, a must-have head covering for a ten-year-old boy. No doubt the clothing fad originated with the popular 1936 movie, *Daniel Boone*, starring George O'Brien. At that time, Davy Crockett, noted for his coonskin hat, was merely a gleam in the eye of Walt Disney. The Disney movie, *Davy Crockett, King of the Wild Frontier* wasn't released until 1954. My coonskin cap was made of green cloth and had pull down side earmuffs. On the crown of the cap were stitched three rows of what supposedly was real coonskin. As the final touch of elegance there was a removable raccoon tail attached to the back of the cap. I never did figure out when the tail was to be removed-perhaps when entering a church or other sacred place. This fad didn't last long. If the coonskin part of the cap got soaked in the rain, it emitted a very strange odor for several hours until it dried.

Another popular headgear for a ten-year-old boy was the leather skullcap. It was a cross between a beanie and a Yarmulke. Spanky McFarland and Wheezer popularized this headgear in the *Our Gang* comedies. We saw Spanky and the gang movies every Saturday morning at the Uptown Theater. Spanky was never without his cap, nor were we. We used to embellish the cap with various pins, a popular fad. We all wore the Red Cross button, the Children's Museum membership pin and the Audubon Society membership pin, all acquired at grade school for a small cash donation to join the organization. We added other pins, ranging from 1940 presidential campaign buttons to Little Orphan Annie, Moon Mullins, and Harold Teen comic buttons.

We all carried a rabbit's foot and a lucky coin in our pant pockets, although we didn't know anyone who had been blessed with good luck by doing so. The coin we carried could be either a hard-to-find Indian head penny minted through 1908, or a thin, elongated Lincoln head penny that had been flattened on a streetcar or railroad track.

Another popular fashion of the late 1930s was wearing a live chameleon on the shirt lapel. The chameleon was a gray-green lizard, three to four inches long, which remained motionless for long periods of time, and required very little food according to an ad in one of our favorite magazines, *Open Road for Boys*. The lizard had the added attraction of being able to change its skin color. We were warned not to put the lizard on a plaid background, or it might try to change colors so quickly that the chameleon would explode. We purchased the chameleons at Danner Brothers in Broad Ripple. We had tried guppies and goldfish as house pets, but they were just too boring, penned up either in an indoor aquarium or outdoors in a fishpond. With the lizard and its food supply in hand, we were ready for the public showing. We fashioned a small tether out of a piece of ribbon and secured it around the chameleon's neck and to the shirt with a safety pin. We could hardly wait to get to school with our portable pets. The one saving factor was that the lizard stayed on the shirt in one position for hours at a time. A few of the teachers tolerated our wearing the chameleon, as long as doing so didn't disrupt the class.

The least expensive and most popular creature to carry to school was the Mexican Jumping Bean. In essence the small bean acted as an enclosed cage for what purported to be a live creature inside, a small moth larva that could rock and roll. The unexpected movement of the beans fascinated us, but no one ever opened one of the beans to see if there really was a live worm inside. Rumor had it that many of the Mexican Jumping beans were fakes and contained only a single copper BB gun shot.

I usually walked home for a lunch of Campbell's tomato soup and white bread spread with a thick layer of peanut butter and grape jelly along with a glass of whole milk. The only variation on the lunch theme was the occasional Kraft's pimento cheese sandwich, together with a bowl of Campbell's chicken-noodle soup. The empty pimento cheese container doubled as a fruit juice glass. On inclement days we were allowed to take a sack lunch to school. Of course there wasn't a school cafeteria, so we had to eat lunch in our homeroom, under the tight scrutiny of our teacher.

Our teachers instilled in us the spirit of competition, which I still value as a worthwhile trait. For example in the seventh grade math class, we had to calculate the answers to eight problems: two addition, two subtraction, two division and two multiplication. At the teacher's signal, we tried to solve the eight problems as quickly as possible. The hook was that as soon as we had finished, we had to hand carry the test up to the teacher in front of the class. It didn't take us very long to sort out the fast kids from those not so fast. We tried our hardest not to be one of the last ones to finish.

HOLIDAY HIGHLIGHTS

In grade school there were several holidays in the school year when we exchanged greeting or friendship cards. On Valentine's Day, we handmade cards at school to pass out to our classmates. There was no requirement about how many cards each student was to hand out or to whom. As usual, the popular kids received the greatest number of cards. Popularity then was defined for girls as the cutest ones and for boys as the most athletic. The rest of us always hoped that next year would be different.

In the early years every December Mary Ellen and I wrote notes to Santa in care of the North Pole. As a youngster I loaded up my wish list with all sorts of goodies ranging from lead soldiers to a Buck Rogers ray gun and Tinker Toys to Lincoln logs. I knew that I wouldn't receive everything I wanted but didn't want to leave anything out. I also knew that I would see Santa in person at Blocks Department Store right before Christmas. He undoubtedly would ask me if I had been a good boy and I didn't want to disappoint him. The day finally arrived when we boarded the College Avenue streetcar with Mom for the ride downtown. It was time to have a chat with Santa at Block's. Sure enough we had our chance to meet the big man after what seemed like a lifetime waiting in line. When he asked me what I wanted for Christmas I was rather surprised. After all I had sent him a personal letter with my want list a few weeks earlier. Had my letter been lost in the mail? Had he forgotten what I wanted? Just to play it safe I whispered the list to him verbatim.

Several days before Christmas I had been warned by Mom that I had better straighten up right away or Santa might leave a lump of coal in my stocking instead of the toys I had asked him for. Now I had seen hundreds of pictures of Santa with a large bag of toys slung over his back and never once had I seen him carrying a bag of coal. However, I realized that at our house Santa could walk down just one flight of stairs to our basement coal bin which was overflowing with the hard black stuff. There he could have the pick of the lot to put in my stocking hung by the chimney with care. Since it was not wise to take chances with Santa, I was on my best behavior until right after Christmas day. Sure enough on the big day I did receive several of the requested items from Santa.

With two weeks off from school over the Christmas recess there was plenty of time for fun activities such as snowball fights. By that time in our young lives we had tired of making snow men and snow forts. As with other kid activities, there were inviolate rules for snowball fights that varied from neighborhood to neighborhood. First the battle lines had to be drawn. In our neighborhood the alley behind our house on Park Avenue was the battle zone for war with the Central Avenue boys on the adjacent street. Second, it was agreed that no rocks would be used inside the snowballs; it all had to be hand work. Third, it was permissible to use the lid of any neighbor's metal garbage can found in the alley as a shield. Fourth, no girls were allowed at the battle scene and most importantly, no parents were to be told about the fight. Usually the fights ended in a draw with both sides declaring victory and the only casualties a few frost bitten hands and a body ache or two from well aimed missiles.

July Fourth was my favorite holiday of the year after Christmas. The sky was literally the limit as far as fireworks were concerned, since there were no laws prohibiting igniting any explosive devices, no matter how dangerous. We boys woke up early on the Fourth to the sound of firecrackers exploding throughout the neighborhood. We quickly gathered with our fireworks and punk from caches scattered throughout the neighborhood. Punk was a flammable fiber-like substance molded onto a long wooden stick, which was used to light the fireworks. The advantage of the punk sticks over matches or a cigarette lighter was that once lit, the punk smoldered for several minutes and could be used over and over again without relighting.

Keeping a safe distance was vital when attempting to relight a firecracker whose fuse had burned only part way down the first time. We called this scenario "relight the shorter fuse and run like hell." Our favorite firecracker was the cherry bomb. It was unique in that it exploded under water. Many a backyard goldfish pond felt the shock wave of a tossed cherry bomb with no doubt a significant loss of fish life.

Another firecracker we liked was the ladyfinger, which was usually exploded as packaged in a long string of fifty to one hundred braided crackers. The individual crackers were only one half inch long and about the circumference of a large wooden kitchen match. The more adventuresome guys unbraided the mass of ladyfingers and exploded them individually as follows: A single tiny unbraided firecracker was placed firmly between the thumb and index finger and held out at arms length. If all went well when the tiny firecracker was ignited, the force of the explosion did not backfire into the holder's hand.

Other fireworks we enjoyed were pinwheels, skyrockets, fountains, and torpedoes. The torpedoes were perhaps the most dangerous, since they exploded on contact with any hard surface. Just throw and go. There was no fuse to light as with firecrackers. The torpedo, a shiny silver metallic looking round explosive, even smelled dangerous. Many boys had minor leg burns from engaging in torpedo duels. Such a wound was considered a red badge of courage.

For the faint of heart, we bent two one-inch firecrackers in half, enough to expose their gunpowder. When the two firecrackers were placed facing each other and lit with a piece of punk, the resulting duel of burning powder was surprisingly fun to watch. For the very young there were always sparklers and snakes, which were non-explosive and quite harmless, but for the older boys those were boring!

There was talk around the neighborhood that we could make our own real July 4th firecrackers. Rumor had it that the Gilbert Chemistry set had all of the necessary ingredients. Rhude and I pooled our money and purchased one of the less expensive Gilbert sets, which featured forty different chemicals, including what we thought were the necessary ingredients. The chemicals were stored in small glass bottles and vials with neat looking technical labels. The set also included test tubes and racks, litmus paper, beakers, eyedropper, alcohol lamp burner and most importantly a lengthy experiment instruction manual. We read the instruction manual from cover to cover but couldn't find a formula for making gunpowder. It was a great disappointment to us, since we assumed that the Gilbert slogan "Fun with Chemistry" meant their booklet included instructions for making explosives. We did find out later that the drugstore sold all the necessary ingredients to make gunpowder over the counter, so there had been no real need to buy the chemistry set in the first place.

Perhaps the most ubiquitous and harmless noisemaker associated with the Fourth of July was the cap gun. We never heard of anyone being hurt by shooting one; it was the one noisemaker used all year round. The cap gun was heavily featured in the game of Cowboys and Indians, our game of choice because of the radio program the *Lone Ranger* and cowboy movie serials with such stars as Johnny Mack Brown and Hopalong Cassidy. Our cowboy outfits usually consisted of a single-shot cap gun stuck in our regular trouser belt and what passed for a cowboy hat. If we were to be Indians, we painted stripes on our faces with black shoe polish and some of our Moms' rouge. We then stuck some fake turkey feathers into a headband and carried a long bladed rubber knife in our belt. To finish off the outfit, we either made or borrowed another kid's bow and arrow set. As Indians we never actually shot real arrows at the pretend enemy, but rather shouted out words like "got'cha, you're dead." The cowboys used more realistic weapons because their cap guns made real noises. For some reason, the Indians never won our game just like they never won in the Saturday afternoon cowboy serials at the Uptown Theater.

MARAUDING INDIAN BRAVE

The Fourth of July holiday usually included an afternoon picnic at one of our favorite parks. This was followed by an evening drive to the outdoor Butler Bowl at 49th and Boulevard Place to watch the professional fireworks extravaganza.

Another noisy night was on New Year's Eve when we celebrated the arrival of the coming year at home. It was the one night we children were allowed to stay up until midnight. Starting at 9:00 PM the family huddled around the radio and listened as the New Year was welcomed on the hour in distant places. Finally it was midnight and our turn to celebrate. As the radio strains of Auld Lang Syne played by the wailing saxophones of Guy Lombardo's Royal Canadians rang in our ears, we raced out onto the front porch. There Mary Ellen and I made a deafening noise with leftover Halloween noisemakers and banging old tin pie pans together. Our neighbors joined in the din with their firecrackers and carbide canons. Now Dad joined in the celebration with his very own noise maker, a Civil War Remington pistol. He had purchased the gun in Arizona in 1912 to add to his collection of old firearms. His gun hobby started as young man when he and his two brothers had a collection of Civil War weapons which they enjoyed handling and drilling with. He limited his use of fire-arms to target practice and didn't hunt live game. Dad said that he had quite enough of that type of blood sport when he served overseas in the military during World War I.

One New Year's Eve Dad loaded all six cylinders of the old Civil war revolver with black powder as usual but also installed all six of the primer caps immediately rather then individually before each shot was fired. Unfortunately when the hammer struck the first primer cap, the flash-over ignited all five other primer caps and all six charges of powder went off simultaneously. Dad's scorched hands and arms convinced him never to try that stunt again.

CLASSROOM MONITORS

Part of the learning process at PS 84 was the informal monitor-ing system. A few children were selected by their teachers for class monitors. Their duties included passing out the teacher's lesson plan for the day and any homework assignment and copying the weekly school newsletter on the mimeograph machine. This system built self-esteem for the chosen few and developed in them a heightened sense of responsibility. The rest of us begrudgingly acknowledged that the monitors were usually the smartest kids in the class. You know, they were the type who were first to raise a hand when the teacher asked a question about homework or asked for a volunteer to read a short passage from *Gulliver's Travels*. They were the kids who memorized all of the verses to a poem, not just the assigned first verse. They never needed to use an eraser when working math problems at the black-board. We lumped all of the monitors together as teachers' pets.

Every day, each classroom had two monitors assigned to clean the chalk erasers. The dirty erasers were carried outside to the rear schoolyard where they were banged together to get rid of the dust. Some of the more enterprising boys banged individual erasers against the back wall of the school building to clean them. Although we had been warned not to do so, I thought of it as a creative outlet since the chalk dust did form some interesting patterns on the school's red brick walls.

Another classroom honor was raising and lowering the large windows on hot days in May, early June, September, and October. There was no mechanical air conditioning at school, or at home for that matter. The window monitor used the seven-foot pole with a metal hook on one end to reach up, engage the latch, and lower the upper window. The reverse procedure was used near the end of the school day.

A student monitor rang the school chimes throughout the day to announce the start of each class period. The stand that held four long brass chimes was strategically placed outside of the principal's first floor office, assuring that no student attempted to ring the chimes at the wrong time.

First through fourth grade classrooms were located on the first floor, along with the principal's office, the nurse's office, the teachers' lounge, and the combination auditorium and gymnasium. It was a rare day when a younger student dared venture up to the off-limits second floor. We all looked forward to that day when we became fifth graders and could legitimately roam the second floor. One of the perks of having a second floor homeroom was using the four foot high water fountains, unlike the shorter ones on the first floor. By the time we were big fifth graders, it would have been humiliating to do a deep knee bend in order to get a drink of water out of the kiddy fountains. On the second floor, each major subject was taught by a different teacher in her own classroom. There was a separate teacher for English and spelling, reading and writing, science and math, social studies, geography and history, music, and one who taught art, health, safety, and gym.

Another monitor assignment was the milk and cracker brigade. Each day at 10:00 AM classes took a short recess for a snack. The choices were a half pint of white or chocolate milk (in glass bottles not waxed cardboard cartons) and graham or soda crackers. The cost was five cents. The monitors set up the tables at the end of each hall, with the help of the seldom-seen janitor, and loaded them with milk and two large cracker boxes. When the break was over, the monitors helped repack the leftover milk and crackers and put them away. The best part of the job was to nibble on the few broken crackers during the recess.

Another important monitor daily duty was raising and lowering the American flag by two upperclassmen who were usually traffic boys. They were taught the proper respect for the flag and the proper method of unfolding and folding it. They also made sure the flag never touched the ground during the ceremony.

A large number of student monitors was required to set up and take down chairs to accommodate the three hundred plus student body during school assembly. The chairs were set up in the combination gymnasium/auditorium, where such activities as music recitals by the student orchestra, junior high choir presentations, and student plays were held. The hardwood floors were always freshly waxed, and we were cautioned to walk on them with care. No sliding of chairs during the auditorium set-up! One day during a chair set-up session, Bill Slacker decided to try and see how far he could slide on the newly waxed floors in his "clodhopper" shoes. Those popular heavy-duty shoes were high top and had thick soles. When Miss Gallagher, the gym teacher in charge of the task, saw what happened, she whipped the heavy nickel-plated whistle off her neck and hit him across the face with the lanyard. Bill never tried to slide on the floors again.

Perhaps the greatest honor of all was being the principal's errand monitor. The student selected was given simple chores in the principal's office and also ran errands around the school such as taking notes to the teachers. I was never so honored although I did spend a considerable amount of time at the principal's office. It was on a cold, hard bench reserved for special students. The teacher was the first line of punishment for special students, those who had caused a problem in the classroom. Often the punishment was requiring the student to sit inside the teacher's kneehole desk opening. The length of stay in the "cage" varied from teacher to teacher and infraction to infraction. If the student was a recidivist offender he was sent to the principal's bench for re-indoctrination. The bench was strategically placed so that the offender was in plain view of all the kids walking by at class break. Needless to say we received many nasty comments and funny faces. After an agonizing wait, the principal took over and gave us a stern lecture.

TRAFFIC BOYS ON PATROL

Almost all of the seventh grade boys were selected as traffic boys and were considered by the school as part of the unofficial police department. It was quite an honor to be inducted into such an elite organization. At the induction ceremony, the captain of the traffic patrol boys, Warren Rich, handed each neophyte a bright shiny badge and a white safety belt to wear. With the requirement that the white traffic belt always look clean was the recommendation that the belt be washed at least once a week. However, right before weekly inspection, some of the guys used classroom chalk to whiten their unwashed belts when no one was looking. The traffic boys' main duty was as crossing guards at those busy intersections where children were on their way to or from school.

In the eighth grade I was finally considered responsible enough to be a traffic boy. My assignment was to hold back the eager bike riders at the end of the school driveway at three in the afternoon when school was dismissed. The other traffic post located on the school grounds was at the front entrance to the school. That post required two traffic boys to stand back to back and blow bugles as loudly as possible in opposite directions five minutes before school was to start each morning, as an early warning system for lingering students to get to school on time. In those days wristwatches were a fairly new item and far too expensive for most parents to give their children to wear to school.

Another traffic boy duty was keeping an eye out for possible lawbreakers. Three serious infractions that resulted in a visit to school traffic court were running across a guarded street rather than walking, stepping off the sidewalk into the street between corners, and walking on someone's lawn. The offender, often a first to fourth grader, was hauled into traffic court (one of our upper grade classrooms) filled with traffic boys and presided over by the captain of the traffic boys. There Miss Gallagher, head of the traffic patrol who also served as the gym teacher, lectured the tearful, trembling child. Before leaving the court room, the child had to promise that the infraction would never, never happen again.

A fun day away from teachers and studies for some of the older boys was working on the semi-annual school paper drive. The night before the paper drive a long-bed truck delivered empty wood slat containers to the school. The crates were about four feet wide, four feet high and eight feet long. The containers were positioned in the street in front of the school, to be picked up full of discarded papers and magazines the next evening. On the morning of the paper drive, some parents dropped off a carload of newspapers and magazines that their children had collected in the neighborhood. In those instances where the papers were not dropped off at the school, they were picked up at designated houses in the neighborhood by those mothers who knew how to drive and had access to a car. Some of the boys rode with the moms to help load and unload the papers. Other boys remained at the school dumpsite and waited for the next carload of newspapers.

When things were quiet and no cars were waiting in line, those of us working at school climbed into the partially filled paper containers to search for interesting magazines. After we had glanced at them, we usually threw them back on the pile. Our version of risqué pictures was in the readily available *Pageant* magazine. It often had color photos of attractive young ladies wearing what was then considered quite daring—ample two-piece bathing suits. In the1930s men as well as women were still required to wear bathing suits that covered their entire torso. That is, if they wished to swim in the Indianapolis Parks Department pools. In 1937, an article with an accompanying photograph in the local newspaper stated that three young men were ordered to leave an Indianapolis municipal pool because they were not wearing a top to their bathing suits.

During one paper drive, the captain of the traffic boys and I borrowed a few comics to take home and read. Somehow the principal found out and called us in for a chat. After we had confessed to taking the magazines, the principal made us promise that as soon as we returned home that afternoon after school, we would throw the comic books in the trash. Sure I did!

TEACHER TALES

Classrooms in our school typically had as many as thirty five to forty students with only one teacher and no helpers. The need to correct student behavior in such a classroom setting was minimal due to strong teacher discipline and parental influence. The working rule at home was "You get in trouble at school and you will rue the day!" Keep in mind that all of our twenty elementary school teachers were women, most of them older no-nonsense types, as was our unsmiling but kindly principal, Miss Elizabeth Scott.

Most of the older teachers wore what amounted to an old lady's uniform. It consisted of a dark dress, shoes and stockings, and little make-up or jewelry. Topping off this uniform several of the teachers wore rimless glasses on a long pull chain. Whenever one of the older teachers wished to make a particularly salient point, she slowly pulled out her pince-nez, perched the eyeglasses on her nose, and peered over them. Such was the case with Miss Belle Inglis, my third grade teacher who was a tiny, white haired grandmotherly-looking woman and my favorite teacher in elementary school. She seemed to take a real interest in us children perhaps because she never had any of her own. Miss Inglis was a successful teacher maybe because she had one teaching technique that differed from any other teachers. She had probably read in a book that children could be motivated by giving them a little recognition for work well done.

Miss Ingles' idea of a tangible reward was to stamp our homework papers with the likeness of a cartoon character of the period. Since the Walt Disney movie *Snow White and the Seven Dwarfs* had been released just a couple of years earlier, she used their likenesses on our papers. If Miss Inglis was pleased with the homework, the girls' papers were stamped with a picture of Snow White while the boys' papers were stamped with Prince Charming. I thought she would probably use the image of the seven dwarfs as well at some point in time. I dreaded getting back a paper with the likeness of Grumpy, but I never did nor did any other student. However, once I did receive back a homework paper stamped with the likeness of Snow White's step mother, the evil queen. I never could figure out what that was all about. Was Miss Inglis trying to tell me something? Was it some sort of a subliminal message? I will say that Miss Inglis must have been on the right track with her teaching methodology since my grades in her class were the best I ever received in elementary school. I looked forward to the parent-teacher night when my Mom and Dad visited Miss Inglis's class. I knew that all would be well when they had a brief chat with her as to my progress.

Two of my upper grade teachers will also forever remain in memory. I will never forget seventh grade science teacher Mrs. Strob, a kindly, short, full-figured, elderly woman who wore her gray hair in a tight bun. She usually wore a long sleeved dark dress that buttoned up the front with a high neckline. She often had a cold and dabbed at her nose daintily with a small hankie. Since her dresses typically had no pockets she was forced to find another hiding place for her hankie. When not in use, Mrs. Strob discretely stuffed the hankie inside her dress front somewhere between the upper and lower buttons. The fun began when she tried to make a point about an esoteric law of science with one hand at the blackboard and at the same time fish for her hankie with the other hand. Often it took her several tries to retrieve the hankie from her bodice, and we students heaved a sigh of relief.

In eighth grade, rumor had it that our gym teacher Miss Gallagher, a no-nonsense, hard looking single lady, had been seen by one of the guys coming out of a Broad Ripple liquor store. What was more shocking was that she was supposedly carrying a six-pack of beer. It was hard to believe that she had stooped so low. After all, she was in charge of the traffic boys and more importantly was also the school liaison with the Indianapolis Police Department. The closest I came to seeing any woman drink an alcoholic beverage was when I brought Mrs. Schenzel that daily dose of "cough remedy" from the drug store one summer. I had never actually seen a woman drink any liquor in real life, including my mother. Mom never had that first of drop of alcohol during her ninety-two year life, not even a sip of champagne at my wedding.

I still feel uncomfortable to this day thinking about those female teachers and principal. A stern look from any one of them could mow down a row of corn stalks twenty paces away. We lived in mortal fear of them. As far as we kids were concerned there were two categories of people living on the planet, human beings and teachers. The teacher's job was to teach; ours was to learn, period. We never thought about them in a personal way. Were they married? Did they have children of their own? Did they have health problems? Did they really enjoy teaching? The teachers in turn never talked about anything except the lesson plan for the day, but they must have done something right at our school. Two U.S. Senators attended PS 84 during the 1930s and 1940s. Other notable individuals in medicine, government, law, and the arts graduated from there as well.

There was one male instructor in school, but he was not part of the main stream teaching curriculum. All boys in the seventh and eighth grades took industrial arts, a fancy name for shop. Mr. Pritchard, the instructor, was easier going and more soft-spoken than most of the lady teachers, and he always had a ready joke. The course work included mechanical drawing, woodwork, metal work, and print shop. Before graduating, every boy was expected to make a small wooden tabletop ironing board for his mother, with which she could iron dresses and shirtsleeves. A small table lamp was made for the father's desk. The older girls had to take home economics, a fancy name for cooking and sewing. Their class was conducted in a specially designed second floor classroom down the hall from our shop class. We boys were never allowed to venture in there and probably would not have done so if allowed.

The only other man in the building was the school janitor who was a mystery since we seldom saw him during our days at school. We heard that he spent most of his day in the basement boiler room, either sleeping or stoking the coal fired furnace, and that he only surfaced after school hours to clean the classrooms.

The teachers didn't frisk us for concealed weapons at the door of the schoolhouse in those days so it wasn't unusual for some upper-class boys to carry such items into the classroom. There were two easily concealed weapons of choice. The first was a small magnifying glass about three inches long; the second was a four-inch long plastic tube water gun.

We had been introduced to the power of the magnifying glass in our seventh grade science class, where we learned that it could concentrate the rays of the sun into a powerful beam of energy. We were anxious to put that scientific principle to practical use. One warm, sunny day, we went out the back door during lunch break to where the kids' bikes were parked. Wanting to try a field experiment with the magnifying glass, we selected one particular bicycle that belonged to a classmate who was a teacher's pet and also a snitch. He had violated several unwritten kid rules and had to receive his just retribution. With one classmate as a lookout, the magnifying glass was positioned at just the right height above the leather seat, and held there until a small hole was scorched in the seat. This hot seat treatment was done only on rare occasions to a boy who had fallen out of favor with his classmates.

To prove that we were equal opportunity pranksters, we used the second weapon on girls only. The long plastic tube, about one-inch in diameter, worked like a water pistol. There was a cork at one end and a small hole in the other end. When the tube was filled with cold water and squeezed, it emitted a long, narrow stream at the unsuspecting victim. The beauty of the weapon was that it could easily be concealed in the hand without anyone's notice. At class break the tube was filled at the nearest water fountain, and then it was time to go on the prowl. When the designated female target walked by, a girl who we thought was snooty, one of the shooters nonchalantly fell into lock step a few paces behind her. At the right moment he aimed for that vital area, the back of her bare legs. When the trigger was squeezed, the shooter ducked into a classroom before his victim turned around.

For us budding teenagers, a popular party theme was the scavenger hunt. Before the hunt we assembled at a classmate's home early on a Saturday evening. After a brief time-out for cake and ice cream, the boys and girls were paired off and handed a list of items to find and bring back to the party house. The rules were simple. Whoever brought back all of the required items first in the allotted time won the game. If no team found all of the items, the team that brought back the most items on the list won. The idea was to canvas the local neighborhood by knocking on every door and trying to convince the homeowner that if they handed over one of the desired items, they would get it back that night. Some of the typical items on the scavenger list were an Indian head penny, a photograph of a cat, a piece of mail with a two-cent stamp (first class postage went to three cents in 1932) and a race-car playing piece used in the early Monopoly board games.

TRIPS NEAR AND FAR

As part of a seventh grade class project for the upcoming presidential election in the fall of 1944, classmate Marty Dayan and I rode our bikes downtown to the Republican campaign headquarters. We picked up several campaign buttons for Wendell Willkie, the Republican candidate for president from Elwood, Indiana. A few of the buttons found their way into my personal collection.

Our one major school outing over the years was the annual trek to the Children's Museum, at the time located in the old Carey mansion at 1150 North Meridian St. I remember being ushered through an old, dimly lit house, crowded on three floors with glass cases filled with old, dead things. Right before visiting the museum, we were encouraged to become members for the current year. In exchange for a small contribution, we were given an official membership button, featuring the picture of a sea horse. I wondered about using something from the ocean as the symbol for the Children's Museum or any other local organization, since Indianapolis had the distinction of being the largest land-locked city in the U.S.

Every summer we Boy Scouts looked forward to a two-week stay at Camp Chank-Tun-Un-Gi. The camp was located on the east side of Indianapolis along Fall Creek near Fort Benjamin Harrison. Our Troop 90 newsletter in May 1945 posted the headline "Camp Offers Swell Time to Rookies." I was to graduate from PS 84 the next month and thought that scout camp would be fun after so much schooling. Once at camp after morning bugle reveille and a hearty breakfast, our days were filled with learning practical things like how to start a fire without using matches and how to blaze a trail with the official Boy Scout hatchet, which was worn in a real leather scabbard on the hip. We were told that those skills would come in handy when we returned home from camp. However I was not convinced of their usefulness. I thought if you want to start a fire why not just borrow a cigarette lighter from your dad or use kitchen matches that strike on any surface. Also, who needed to blaze a trail? Wouldn't the neighbors be upset if we hacked up their trees to mark our way home? There were also classes in boating, swimming and life saving. After dinner we sat around the campfire singing such songs as "Old MacDonald Had a Farm." Skits and games followed the songfest.

The camp experience was considered a success only if we came home with the Firecrafter patch to proudly display on our uniforms. The patch was awarded to those scouts who displayed the proper attitude, set examples for other scouts to follow, showed respect to other campers and showed respect for the environment. Although I received the Firecrafter patch, it didn't help matters that I had to be ignobly towed back to shoreline when I was boating on Fall Creek. The water level was low due to a recent drought, and I stranded my rowboat on some large rocks in the middle of the creek. After a few calls for help, I was rescued to the accompaniment of many hoots and hollers from those scouts on the shoreline. Apparently it didn't help my boating skills that I knew all of the words to "Row, Row, Row Your Boat."

The food at camp was unforgettable. That is where I was introduced to and grew to loathe apple butter. It was served to us morning, noon and night. I remember how one of the kitchen helpers opened loaves of bread by banging on one end of the loaf with his closed fist. If he did it just right, the bread wrapper virtually exploded and split the loaf into two flattened sections. We had to use the resulting deformed bread for our apple butter sandwiches. Years later the Camp Chank-Tun-Un-Gi name was changed to Camp Belzer, no doubt because no one could pronounce the former name, much less spell it.

Returning after summer camp to our regular Boy Scout meeting at Broadway Evangelical Church at 56th and Broadway Streets, I was approached by the Scoutmaster for a little chat. He reminded me that I had never advanced beyond the rank of Second Class Scout, which was only one step up from that dreaded neophyte designation Tenderfoot. Also, he reminded me that I had the rather dubious distinction of holding the Second Class rank longer than anyone else in our troop. My problem was that I had never learned to swim, which was a requirement for the next rank of First Class Scout. By mutual agreement with the Scoutmaster, I was out of the troop for good. That ignominious departure left an indelible impression on me at the time since all of my friends were still in the troop. I was now an outsider.

Although my tenure as a Boy Scout was cut short through unfortunate circumstances, I did manage to acquire a few merit badges along the way. My favorite was the Pioneering badge. Among other requirements to earn that badge was learning how to tie a series of knots that would come in handy in the wilderness. Dad jumped at the chance to help me with the project. During his World War I naval training, he had learned to tie many different knots. He in turn taught me how to tie the half hitch, bowline, sheepshank and single carrick bend. These knots and several other types made out of clothesline were labeled and mounted on a plaque made from the end of a dismantled orange crate. That knot plaque hung proudly in my bedroom for many years.

One thing I did take away from Scouting was the fine art of Indian hand wrestling. What appealed to me about this non-contact sport was that it required no equipment, could be done anywhere and didn't require much energy. As scouts we learned that several American Indian tribes had engaged in various forms of wrestling of which hand wrestling was one of the more popular. To engage in this sport two boys stand right foot next to right foot facing each other. Their right hands are clasped, left feet braced and left hands behind the back. At the signal "Go" each combatant tries to unbalance the other by pulling, pushing or twisting their opponent's right arm. The first contestant to move either foot loses the game. To this day I enjoy the sport and am still willing to take on all comers.

Perhaps our greatest adventure during elementary school was an out of state trip sponsored by Tabernacle Presbyterian Church. Their annual trek to far off places occurred during the school holiday for the State Teacher's Convention. In October 1944, fifty kids climbed on the bus for a trip to the Kentucky tourist sites of Stephen Foster's My Old Kentucky Home, Ft. Knox, (we saw the gold!), and Mammoth Cave. It was at the cave that I learned the difference between a stalactite and a stalagmite. Unfortunately this newly found knowledge didn't fit into our guys' usual conversation about bikes, babes and baseball.

TABERNACLE PRESBYTERIAN CHURCH–1945 ROAD TRIP

AUTOGRAPH BOOKS

In those days, almost every kid owned and used an autograph book. They came in handy in those rare situations when one of our grade school classmates moved away. The departing signature was usually accompanied by a snappy poem or saying such as "You are 2-good, 2-be, 4-gotten." Many other autograph verses were popular at the time in grade school. (See Appendix.)

As we reached our teen-age years the autograph books came in handy once again, when we heard the big bands play at the downtown Circle Theater. Of course the first stop was at Morrow's Nut House at the corner of Market and Pennsylvania Streets for a twenty five cent bag of hot cashews. I always liked their slogan *"Nuts to You."* After the show we waited patiently at the stage door clutching our autograph books, in hopes that the bandleader or one of the featured vocalists such as Ginny Simms or Francis Langford would appear. Some of the more popular bands that included Indianapolis in their national tours were Kay Keyser and his Kollege of Musical Knowledge (starring Ish Kabibble), Horace Height and his Musical Knights, Benny Goodman, the King of Swing, and Sammy Kaye with his Swing and Sway.

Looking back at my autograph book, the most impressive sentiment expressed on those pages was by a grade school teacher who wrote, "O lad be strong and rightly learn to choose. The world is yours and all it holds to use." I am sure that she wrote the same passage in all of my schoolmates' autograph books over the years, but I wonder if one of my schoolmates in particular really paid attention to the poem's message. His name was Edward Hilgemeier Jr. and his family owned a large pork packing firm in Indianapolis, Hilgemeier and Brother.

Eddy's fifteen minutes of fame came ten years after he left School 84. He was selected as a backup contestant for one of the popular daytime TV quiz programs called *Dotto*, filmed in New York City. While waiting to be selected, Eddie innocently picked up a notebook which a prior contestant had left behind in the studio waiting room. The book contained the answers to the very questions that were posed to the same contestant that evening. When Eddie took the book to another contestant who had just been defeated on that show, they decided to confront the show's producer, who admitted that in the past, contestants had been given answers to questions which were asked on the next show. Eddie and the other contestant agreed to remain silent in exchange for a cash payment. When Eddie, who received fifteen hundred dollars, found out that the other contestant was given four thousand dollars, he went to the state Attorney General's office. Later a well-known game show contestant corroborated Eddie's story. As a result of the official investigation, the reputations of all involved as well as the game show format itself were severely damaged.

The fallout spread to other quiz shows where many contestants came under suspicion as well. Included in the growing scandal was one of the top quiz show contestants of the day, Charles Van Doren, a professor of English at Columbia University. His national reputation led to being featured on a *Time Magazine* cover in 1957. Soon thereafter in front of a grand jury, he denied being involved in any quiz show cheating. However, in 1959 he finally confessed to the charade, losing his teaching position at Columbia University as a result.

A 1994 movie, *Quiz Show,* chronicled Van Doren's rise and fall in the 1950s TV quiz show world.

Shortridge High School

Most of the children in our neighborhood went to Broad Ripple High School which was the closest to our house, but I chose Shortridge since my best grade school chum, Richard Rhude, and my sister Mary Ellen liked the school. Shortridge High School had a storied past. It started in 1864 as Indianapolis High School, and was the first public high school in the city. In 1899, its name was changed to Shortridge. Over the years its accomplishments have been many and varied. They range from being the first high school in the country to publish a daily student paper, *The Daily Echo,* starting in 1899, to having its own radio station, WIAN, which commenced operation in 1954. In 1947, Shortridge was rated one of the top forty high schools in the country, several of which were private schools. In 1956, the high school became active in the American Field Service program that placed foreign students in American high schools. Shortridge was the high school to go to for those students who wanted to learn since the curriculum ranged from Greek, college algebra, calculus, chemistry, and physics, to fine arts, music, and drama. In the 1940s, graduation from Shortridge High School precluded the need for the better students to take entrance examinations to enroll in most universities.

THE GLAMOUR OF THE UNIFORM

One of the first decisions that I had to make when entering Shortridge was the choice between physical education and ROTC. I opted for the latter. Perhaps it was the glamour of the uniform that caught my fancy or maybe it was the fact that I would be able to fire a real rifle inside the school building. The ROTC, a Shortridge tradition since 1920, had set up a basement firing range for the cadets with 22-caliber rifles and live ammunition. I had always wanted to learn how to shoot a weapon and here was my chance. It was not long before I was proudly wearing the ROTC uniform to school three days a week. At the time I enlisted, I was not aware that ROTC was looked upon with disdain by the in-crowd. They called us ROT-C's with the emphasis on the first syllable. I always thought that the official name sounded much nicer -- the Reserve Officers Training Corps.

After several weeks of ROTC training, including indoor target practice, I became so enthusiastic about the sport that I implored Dad to take me target shooting somewhere outside of the city. Dad owned several weapons including a thirty-year-old single-shot bolt action 22-caliber rifle that had been stored unused in the closet for many years. Up to that point I had only used a BB gun for target practice with Mom's admonition, "Be careful or you will shoot your eye out" ringing in my ears. Little did I realize just how prophetic her comment was when I went target shooting with that 22-caliber rifle for the first time. Finally the day came when Dad drove us to a wilderness area near the entrance to Ft. Benjamin Harrison on the east side of Indianapolis. Against the side of a small hill we set up some old tin cans for target practice. Dad fired his handgun, a Colt Woodsman 22-caliber automatic pistol, while I shot the old 22-caliber rifle.

After I had fired several rounds of ammunition successfully, my rifle misfired. To try again, I pulled the bolt back and then locked it into place a second time against the cartridge. When I squeezed the trigger, there was a loud explosion and the bolt somehow forced its way back out of its housing and flew out to the rear of the rifle. In doing so, the bolt glanced off my right eye and cheek and landed about ten feet behind me. I was stunned and bleeding profusely from the wound. Dad rushed me to the nearest hospital where the wound was stitched up. Fortunately the accident did not damage my right eye seriously. The best part of the story was that I had to wear a black eye patch to high school for several days while the eye was healing. I hoped that I looked like that guy who wore an eye patch in those magazine ads touting a popular brand of Scotch whiskey.

CLASSROOM ANTICS

Shortridge High had its share of dedicated teachers including Mr. Frank B. Wade, my first year chemistry teacher, who was an elderly and friendly gentleman. With his full head of white hair, white mustache, rimless glasses and dark vested suit he looked like a cross between Dr. Albert Schweitzer and Albert Einstein. Mr. Wade walked, talked, and lived chemistry. Even his dress suit was chemistry in action as it often carried traces of chemicals from his recent experiments. Here and there on his lapel was a spot of yellow from an experiment with sulfur; his suit sleeve might have a light red streak from working with iron oxide; or the front of his white dress shirt was dotted with black specs from charcoal compounds. His conversation was laced with chemical equations and experiments and he talked as if the Table of Periodic Elements was an old friend. He was even on a first name basis with the halogen family; namely fluorine, chlorine, bromine, iodine and astatine.

My first day in the chemistry lab was one I will never forget. It was as if I had walked into the laboratory of the mad doctor in the early Frankenstein movies which I enjoyed as a young kid. The pungent smell of chemicals saturated the air. There was lab equipment everywhere: bubbling beakers heated by Bunsen burners, scales, flasks, racks of test tubes, large glass cylinders filled with strange smelling liquids, a microscope or two and what seemed like endless miles of rubber tubing. During that first day Mr. Wade initiated our class into the wonders of chemistry as he had done with so many classes before. We were about to witness first hand a chemical reaction by which one substance is produced from or converted into another substance. To make his point and to get our attention, he gathered us around one of the lab sinks. Without any explanation he dropped a small quantity of an unidentified substance into the sink basin and yelled "duck." When the chemical hit the standing water in the sink there was quite a loud explosion and a cloud of noxious smoke. After the smoke cleared and we students had calmed down, Mr. Wade went on to explain that the chemical which had made the explosion was metallic sodium. Needless to say that chemical was quite unstable when combined with H_2O.

He then recited his favorite story. It seemed that during World War II, a small American freighter with a mixed cargo was caught in a violent Atlantic Ocean storm and was about to be swamped. The captain ordered the crew to throw overboard as much of the cargo as possible to lighten the load which they quickly did. Unfortunately the cargo included several small wooden crates filled with metallic sodium in glass containers. When the crates hit the water, Boom! End of ship and end of story. (It's a dirty shame that sea captain had not taken Mr. Wade's class in chemistry.)

By the end of the school year, to my credit I did retain a few nuggets of knowledge about chemistry. I had learned to balance chemical equations and that Phlogiston really wasn't an element as thought in the Middle Ages. On a practical basis I learned how to boil water and how to make H_2S a.k.a. as hydrogen sulfide which had the smell of rotten eggs. After all, one could never tell when the application of this knowledge might come in handy to a smart, sophisticated young man about town. I also learned how to fashion a neat looking water bottle gun using a glass beaker, cork, and rubber tubing.

CULTURE BEYOND THE CLASSROOM

The high school administration believed in enriching our lives beyond the classroom through frequent appearances of guest performing artists at the school's auditorium, Caleb Mills Hall. There we heard the Indianapolis Symphony Orchestra under the direction of Fabian Sevitzky and the famous tenor opera singer, Lauritz Melchoir. We also heard violin virtuoso "Rubinoff and his Magic Violin," who was somewhat of an egotist and billed himself as "Rubinoff - the Great Violinist." Mind you, Caleb Mills Hall was the same place where we saw movies over the student lunch hour. For a ten-cent admission fee, we could eat our lunch and watch Spanky McFarland and Our Gang, including Alfalfa, Porky and Buckwheat, get into more trouble.

Speaking of educational entertainment, a rite of passage for teenage boys into adulthood was a mandatory visit to one of the local burlesque theaters. In the 1940s downtown Indianapolis featured the Fox and the Mutual burlesque theaters on Illinois Street. The friendly Fox Theater, located at 242 North Illinois Street in the York Hotel building, was the best or the worst depending upon your point of view. The theater wasn't quite as tawdry as the Mutual since its interior wasn't quite as dirty and the rows of wooden seats weren't as likely to collapse when the patrons up front leaned back for a better look at the dancing girls. I remember the first time I visited the Fox Theater I was very nervous. I was afraid that someone in the audience might recognize me and the word would quickly get back to my parents. However after thinking it over, I came to the conclusion that no one else in the audience wanted anyone to know that they were there and consequently I had nothing to worry about.

At the Fox the performance went something like the following: first the house lights were lowered which we believed was done because the "girls" were so unattractive looking. Then the three piece band consisting of a piano player, saxophonist and drummer struck up a lively dance step. This was the signal for the five "local girls" to parade out on the small stage in their abbreviated costumes. When the girls tried to dance in time to the music it looked like the amateur hour in full bloom. A couple of the girls were so heavy that they waddled rather than danced while another looked too old to walk without a cane, much less dance. We figured that the only way the older one managed to get on the stage was as a part owner of the show. The girl's skimpy costumes appeared to be homemade and no doubt covered a multitude of sins. Then one of the local girls was featured doing a so-called solo strip act. More often than not we felt like saying "Keep it on" rather than the usual "Take it off." In any event there was more skin showing at the beach than at the burlesque house. The last act before the break was a comic skit featuring one of the local girls and the house comic appropriately named Scurvy.

At the break, the house lights were turned up and the so-called Master of Ceremonies addressed the audience with his familiar spiel which went something like this: "All right boys, we have a real treat in store for you tonight. Through special arrangements with the supplier we are fortunate to bring you a generous selection of Mother Murphy's salt water taffy. Besides the tasty candy, each and every box is guaranteed to contain one of the following: a Ronson cigarette lighter, an Eversharp pen and pencil set, a Bulova wrist watch or a men's or ladies gift." As an example of a men's gift he might hold up a pair of cheap plastic binoculars. He then proceeded to hold the glasses up to his eyes and turn the viewing adjustment knob. "Guys, these binoculars really magnify. Why with these glasses you can almost touch the girls. Yes, for only twenty five cents, just one quarter of a dollar, this gift and a generous supply of salt water taffy can be yours." This was the signal for the candy butchers to walk up and down the aisles hawking their wares. Once for the fun of it, I purchased a box of the salt water taffy which contained an inexpensive plastic letter opener. Then I surreptitiously took off my inexpensive Waltham wrist watch and held it up in the air for all to see as if I had just found it in my candy box. Without batting an eye or pausing in his spiel, the emcee up front said "See, there goes another Bulova watch to a lucky customer." I always wondered what the emcee really thought at the time since I am sure that he was shocked to see anything of value found in a box of Mother Murphy's Salt Water Taffy.

Then the lights dimmed for the main attraction. The headliner was always a traveling professional strip tease artist who usually did more teasing than stripping. Two of the house favorites were Rose La Rose and Evelyn West. Evelyn according to the emcee had her bosom insured by Lloyds of London for $100,000. She was billed on the marquee as "Evelyn West and her Magic Treasure Chest." Of course our local burlesque house bill of fare could not compare with what was then offered in Calumet City, Illinois known at the time as Sin City, U.S.A., but that is another story.

BASKETBALL HIGHLIGHTS

The most enjoyable part of high school sports for me was attending the annual basketball tournaments at the Butler University Fieldhouse. It was a great remedy for the winter blues. The statewide tournament started with the February sectionals, in which several hundred Indiana high school basketball teams competed throughout the state at selected sites. Then the winners of the sectionals played in statewide regionals, with sixty-four teams competing. The semi-final tournament had sixteen teams competing around the state, and the final four teams played at the Butler Fieldhouse. We faithfully attended every Shortridge basketball game during the tournament. We always hoped we would win our sectional, but it seldom happened.

The 1948-49 Shortridge team was headed by the center Bill Ralph who was six feet five inches tall. As the tallest boy in our high school, he was easy to spot in the hallway during class break. Rumor had it that he had been invited to attend Shortridge by one of the basketball coaches, Jerry Steiner, because Ralph lived outside of the Shortridge school district. During the 1948-49 season, the team had a fair record of eleven wins and seven losses. One of the highlights was a forty five to thirty three win over arch rival Broad Ripple High School. However, the Shortridge Blue Devils were put out of the 1948 sectionals in the second game, suffering a thirty eight to twenty eight loss to cross-town rival, Arsenal Technical High School. Bill Ralph scored all but eight of Shortridges' points in the losing effort.

SUB-DEB DOINGS

High school sub-deb social clubs were popular in those days. In fact the clubs were so popular that *Life Magazine* had a seven-page photographic essay and featured Indianapolis sub-debs in their April 2, 1945, issue. At the time there were seven hundred sub-deb clubs in Indianapolis alone with six thousand members. The *Life* article focused on club initiations and parties. What was more amazing is that *Life Magazine* selected a girl who had just graduated from PS 84 to grace its cover. The cover girl's name was Joan Geisendorff, then a fourteen year-old freshman at Broad Ripple High School. According to the article, she belonged to not one but two sub-deb clubs: the DOR (Daughters of Ripple) and the PAL (Peace and Love).

HIGH SCHOOL HIGH JINKS

I usually rode the bus to high school but occasionally hitchhiked to save the bus fare. Typically, within a few minutes I was able to hitch a ride. One day I was shocked to realize that I was riding with the high school's vice principal who was in charge of school discipline. I had always strived to remain anonymous to anyone in a position of authority. During the ride I was very nervous, although I had never been in any real trouble at school. As it turned out, he didn't ask any questions, was very friendly, and dropped me off in front of the school, saving me bus fare and a four-block walk from the bus stop.

After school was over for the day, we often stood around at Silver's drugstore and told Moron and Knock-Knock jokes. Most adults thought the jokes were corny, but we boys and girls thought that they were neat. The moron jokes had been popular as far back as grade school, when some examples even made it into our eighth grade newspaper. A typical Moron joke went: "Did you hear about the Moron farmer that moved to the city because he heard that the country was at war?" A typical knock-knock joke went: "Knock-Knock," "Who's there?" "Ivan," "Ivan who?" "Ivan awful itchy spot!"

Running out of jokes, we walked across the street from the drug store to Bill Phillip's house to shoot some buckets. The basketball game was played in his driveway where a basketball hoop was mounted on the garage. After a fast paced game, we went inside for a Kool-Aid break. It was time for some fun telephone calls. The guy with the most adult sounding voice called one of the corner drug stores and asked the clerk "Do you have Sir Walter Raleigh in a can?" (It was a popular pipe tobacco of the period.) When the clerk answered in the affirmative, the punch line was "Well you had better let him out or he is going to suffocate in there." A second call placed to another nearby business went: "Is your business located on College Avenue?" "Yes" was the reply, "Well you had better move it off the street quickly because a streetcar is coming!"

Another prank revolved around the trackless trolley that carried students to and from Shortridge High School. For some reason one of my pals had an ongoing feud with an Indianapolis Department of Transportation employee who supervised students boarding the trackless trolley after school. Perhaps the supervisor was upset because my friend continued to repark his junker car in the trolley area reserved for student pickup. This maneuver drove the supervisor wild. As soon as he approached the car to have it moved from the no parking area, my friend pulled his car away from the curb, drove slowly around the block and repeated the procedure.

When this stunt became boring, we decided to embellish it by pretending that the car had broken down in the trolley student pickup area. After a dress rehearsal and the acquisition of the necessary props, we made our move for real. The next time we purposely parked near the trolley boarding area and jumped out of the car to look underneath the hood as if to find the problem. Then we took several tools out of the trunk and pretended to work on the engine, all the while shouting phony instructions to each other and banging on the engine block with hammers to make a lot of noise. Then we threw out a bunch of old auto parts from underneath the hood which had been hidden in the engine compartment the previous evening. When the parts had been strewn around the trolley loading area, we slammed the hood shut, jumped back into the car and pulled away, just as the trackless trolley supervisor approached to find out what was going on. We didn't go back to that trolley stop for a long time.

GAMES OF CHANCE

During high school a favorite teenage pastime was pitching pennies. Several guys met after school in front of Silver's Drug Store with our pockets full of coins. We stood behind a chalk line drawn about eight feet away from the building and pitched the pennies to the point where the wall of the building met the sidewalk. Whoever pitched his penny closest to that point won the round and gathered all of the other pennies in the field of play. This game continued until one or more players were out of change.

Eventually penny pitching lost its luster. Penny-ante poker became our game of choice and chance. Ours was a floating poker game in the sense that the gambling site changed frequently among the few homes where parents allowed such an immoral activity. I remember one game that was scheduled for the home of a classmate whose father was pastor of a local Methodist church. We all knew that Methodists didn't tolerate any form of gambling so we wondered what would happen. As it turned out his parents went out for the evening and left his older brother in charge. All went well since we dealt his brother in on the poker game.

Although we often played the traditional poker games of draw, five-card and seven-card stud, we had three favorites that were a lot more fun. They were Spit-in-the-Ocean, Pass the Trash, and Hi-Lo, Love Thy Neighbor-Costa Muché. The big winner from those high stake poker games might go home with as much as one dollar more than he came with.

Another favorite game of chance was the five-cent pinball machine. Every drugstore had one or more nickel grabber as we called them. If we were able to score enough points, we might win a free game or two. The more enterprising guys tried to elevate the rear of the machine before putting a nickel in the slot. This slowed down the steel pinball as it made its way through the maze of bumpers and scoring posts. Unfortunately most pinball machines had a very sensitive built-in "tilt" mechanism that kicked in to stop the game whenever anyone tried to cheat. We should have listened to that old adage "Cheaters never win."

DRIVE-IN DOINGS

During the late 1940s and early 1950s, the drive-in restaurant became the social icon for teenage drivers with a carload of friends along for the ride. On the north side of Indianapolis there were several drive-ins, each catering to a particular high school student body. The North Pole Drive-In Restaurant at 56th and Illinois St. was the favorite for Broad Ripple High School students. It was also my favorite, although most Shortridge High students hung out at the Ron-D-Vu located just a few blocks away on Westfield Boulevard. The Parkmoor, across from the main entrance to the Indiana State Fairgrounds, and the nearby Teepee Restaurant, each had their own high school fans. On Friday and Saturday nights, the routine was to drive to the four restaurants and slowly circle around each one several times. Hopefully friends were already parked there. After a brief stop for conversation, we moved on to the next drive-in.

The drive-in restaurants typically accommodated two types of customers, each with their own parking area. The serious customers who wanted to get a quick meal and then depart parked in the circle closest to the restaurant building. The back circle was reserved for those teenagers who wanted to park, have a snack, and chat for a long time. The front circle of cars ordered their meals from the girl carhops while the guys and gals in the rear circle usually walked up to the carryout window for their milkshakes or flavored Cokes.

The North Pole was our home away from home. We knew everyone working there, and they knew us. One of my favorite carhops was Marilyn Scoville, also known as Scoop. She was somewhat older than the other carhops, friendly and a real professional. I still remember that when her shift was over for the evening at 1:00 AM, she rode her bike back to her small apartment near 38th and College Avenue; a distance of three miles. She continued to ride a bike to and from work on the evening shift for several years and never had any problem. Several years later Marilyn became the first animal psychiatrist at the Circus-Circus Casino in Las Vegas when it opened in 1968. I am not sure what her educational credentials were for such a job but I do know that she was a true animal lover.

NORTH POLE DRIVE-IN RESTAURANT

We guys spent so much time at the North Pole drive-in that we often received telephone calls from friends or parents while there. Jack Camfield, manager of the restaurant, cooperated to the extent that we could use his business telephone if the calls were short. Fred Morley who owned the restaurant was formerly with the Indiana State Police. His infrequent appearance at the North Pole was akin to the arrival of a visiting head of state. He arrived in a shiny 1937 Pierce Arrow convertible, with the top down whenever possible. Unlike most convertibles, the Pierce Arrow had three rows of seats; a front, rear, and a rumble seat as well. The wheelbase of his 12 cylinder Pierce Arrow was 144 inches long as compared to the usual 1930s car wheelbase of 110-120 inches. That Pierce Arrow was considered to have some of the most advanced styling of any car of the period, with its recessed headlights, elongated hood and streamlined look. As soon as Morley parked the car at the North Pole, he pulled out an extra-long cigarette, inserted it into his gold cigarette holder, and took a deep drag. He was always impeccably dressed in a tailored suit and matching bow tie. He looked as if he had just stepped out of a men's fashion magazine. Once in a great while he donned an old grease-spattered apron and paper hat and worked the hamburger grill while puffing on his cigarette in its long holder. It was an unforgettable scene.

Whenever we decided to leave our home turf to visit a restaurant out in the country, our favorite was Spencer's Restaurant on the far northeast side of Indianapolis near Allisonville Road and Fall Creek Boulevard. We never missed a chance to chat with the greeter as we entered the restaurant. He was a very personable black man who doubled as maitre d' and all around trouble shooter. Although his real name was Eddie Bell, everyone called him Ding Dong, an affectionate nick name. He knew everyone and everyone knew him. As our confidante he could always tell us when any of our friends had been in the restaurant and when they might be returning. In later years Ding Dong became the long serving doorman at the Indiana State Senate in downtown Indianapolis.

At Spencer's we sat around in a large circular booth, "shot the bull," and consumed an inexhaustible supply of fountain Cokes. Our three main interests in life were "souped" up cars, the merits of a particular cheerleader, and the highlights of the most recent high school football or basketball game

Another favorite pastime was watching a movie at one of the drive-in theaters scattered around greater Indianapolis. Our weekly ritual was to pile into Rhude's '37 Chevrolet four door sedan we affectionately called the Log Wagon. If it was a drive-in theater with a per person admission charge, a few of the guys climbed into the large Chevy trunk. After paying admission for the inside passengers, the trunk passengers waited until it was dark and the movie had started and then made their way out of their cramped quarters. The trunk guys sat on the grass to watch the movie since there wasn't enough room for all of us in the car. We wanted to avoid being detected as non-pays by the roving employees or we would all be thrown out en masse.

THAT OLD GANG OF MINE

One of the movies that made the greatest impact on us in our late teens was titled *City Across the River*. It was the story of a gang of guys of a similar age from Brooklyn, NY involved in various delinquent activities. The movie was basically a take off on the Dead End Kids films and starred Tony Curtis in his first screen role. The story line was taken from a popular novel of the period, *The Amboy Dukes*. After seeing the movie we thought it would be fun to organize a gang and call it the 49th Street Boys since several of the guys lived near the corner of 49th Street and Norwaldo Avenue. Just like the Amboy Dukes, we all took on nick names as part of the gang ritual including Bull Baird, Fingers Rhude, Frenchy Featherstone, Meaty Johnson, and Big Boy Booker.

As a high school fringe group, our gang decided to wear modified zoot suits rather than the cords and white dress shirts worn by the in-group. We first heard about zoot suits from news stories surrounding the infamous zoot suit wars in Los Angeles in the summer of 1943. The combatants were the American military versus Mexican-American youths known as Pachucos or Zoot Suiters whose families had been brought into Southern California under the federal Bracero program to work in agriculture. The fight started when a group of American soldiers and sailors claimed they had been assaulted by a gang of Pachucos and swore revenge. Over the next several days a series of pitched battles took place in downtown Los Angeles and East Los Angeles with many on both sides receiving minor injures. By the time the smoke of battle had cleared several hundred Zoot Suiters and nine sailors were arrested for disorderly conduct. After the end of the fracas, the military authorities declared that henceforth the Los Angeles area would be off-limits to all military personnel.

In spite of its shady past, we wore the zoot suit style of clothing which included dress slacks with exaggerated pant legs. These slacks, known as pegged pants, were extra wide at the knees and very narrow at the cuff. In the winter we wore solid colored long sleeve sport shirts in various pastel shades with narrow cloth belts to match. During the warmer months we wore short sleeve shirts outside the slacks. Often a wide brimmed hat and long key chain were added to complete the ensemble.

The radically styled slacks and cloth belts were not available at the local men's clothing stores or at Sears, J.C. Penny or other ready-to-wear retailers, so we went to Lewallen The Tailor in Anderson. Oddly enough, Lewallen not only tailored ladies' and men's clothing but also sold used cars at the same location.

THE CUSTOM CAR CRAZE

As we approached sixteen, the legal age to drive, we boys all dreamed about having a customized car of our own. Unfortunately most of us couldn't even afford a Model A Ford which cost as little as one hundred dollars at the time, so we continued to ride bicycles or find a friend who was lucky enough to own an old car. By the late 1940s the custom car trend was in full swing. It was not unusual for guys to bring their souped up cars to the local drive-in restaurants for all to see. The cars were often owned by boys who had dropped out of high school and gone to work for a living. Often the cars were painted in primer gray with all exterior chrome removed. They often featured Buell air horns, fancy seat covers, dual spotlights, dual exhaust systems, "necker" steering knobs, chrome headlight covers and wind deflectors, fender skirts, sun visors, spinner hubcaps, and leatherette dashboards. Most of these alterations could be done at home, without the services of an expensive professional custom car shop.

One of the wealthier boys, Art Atlas, sported a new 1949 Cadillac Coupe DeVille, which he delighted in showing off at the drive-in restaurants. The car had eight side-by-side rear tail pipes, each of which had a large tail pipe extension called a can. The noise was incredible. The car also had an unusual exhaust odor. In those days it was popular for the car crazies to run their custom cars on a mixture of gasoline and castor oil. The noxious exhaust fumes reminded me of the Indy 500 racecars, which at the time had castor oil added to their gasoline fuel.

Another fad was the installation of spark plugs in the large exhaust cans bolted to the ends of the tail pipes. While the car was running, a switch under the dashboard was turned on and the spark plugs ignited raw gasoline which had been fed into the exhaust pipes. The result was not unlike a flame-thrower, as the flames shot out several feet behind the car.

At home, there wasn't much I could do to customize my first car, a stodgy, black, four-door 1940 Pontiac sedan. The car had originally belonged to Dad who sold it to me when he finally purchased a newer model. As it was, I had to wait several years before I could afford to "customize" a car of my own. By that time the custom car fad had faded and the thrill was gone.

Life In The Outside World

THE GREAT DEPRESSION

In the 1930s, our family listened to President Roosevelt's famous radio fireside chats. Although Dad was a dyed in the wool Republican, he thought that the president had some good ideas when it came to putting people back to work. Roosevelt's aggressive style of officiating galvanized the public into two voting blocks—people either loved him or hated him. His promotion of social issues was unlike any of his predecessors. Added to that was the fact that no one else had ever served more than two terms as president. Roosevelt was vilified by some as a would-be emperor. I remember a 1940 Republican campaign button that called him the Dr. Jeckle of Hyde Park.

In the 1930s, Roosevelt's congressional supporters enacted many back-to-work programs to try and solve some of the economic problems of the Great Depression. The programs were called alphabet soup, since each one had an acronym for the full name of the program. For example, the NRA was the National Recovery Act, the CCC was the Civilian Construction Corps, and the WPA was the Works Projects Administration. Roosevelt's detractors said that the WPA stood for "We Piddle Around." The CCC was acknowledged to be one of the more successful works projects. Young boys from eighteen to twenty three years old were encouraged to join the CCC. They enlisted for a minimum of six months and in return received thirty dollars per month pay, of which twenty-five dollars had to be sent home. Their work is still visible in Indiana State parks where the CCC constructed bridges, trails, park buildings, and fire towers.

During the Great Depression we children were certainly insulated from the problems of the real world. For example, colored people as we called them (this term is still used today—witness the NAACP acronym) were not a part of our daily life. Their plight was never discussed at home, school or mentioned in the newspapers. There weren't any "coloreds" living in our neighborhood or any colored kids in my grade or high school. As a young child I never saw a colored store clerk, policeman, fireman, or bus driver. However, on the radio in the 1930s and 1940s there was one so-called colored program which we enjoyed, the popular long-running comedy series, *Amos and Andy*. Ironically, two white men, Charles Correll and Freeman Gosden, portrayed the radio comedy team although later on television the program had all black actors. The only other show on the air of any prominence to feature a colored main character in the 1940s and 1950s was the radio comedy *Beulah*. Beulah was cast as a colored maid who was portrayed as a one-dimensional servant. She was remembered for her phrases in broken English such as "Love dat man" and "Somebody bawlng fo' Beulah?" The part of Beulah was first played by Marlin Hurt and later Bob Corley, both white men. During the 1930s and 1940s colored screen actresses such as Hattie McDaniels were relegated to minor roles as the quintessential housekeeper or nursemaid. Unfortunately, all too often the colored bit players were cast as uneducated and not very intelligent.

I still remember as a six year old the first colored man I ever saw, on a train ride to Chicago to visit my grandmother. The colored man was a Monon train porter and very friendly. He patted me on the head and told Dad that he should be proud of me for being so well behaved. Dad never grew tired of reminding me of that incident throughout my adolescence. Growing up, most of the colored people I saw in our neighborhood were either cleaning ladies or handymen walking to or from the nearby bus line. During all my adolescent years I never saw a colored person driving an automobile.

As a young teenager there was one colored chap I got to know and respect. His first name was Richard and like me he did odd jobs at Silver's Drug Store at 54th and College Avenue. Richard was a very distinguished looking man who was soft-spoken and quite literate. I imagine that if he had been born 50 years later he might have been a college professor. At Silver's our menial duties included sweeping and moping the floors, taking out trash and sorting returnable empty soda pop and beer bottles by brand in the basement. As a special work assignment, I was trusted to ride my bicycle down to the Fletcher Trust Co. branch at 30th & Illinois to deposit the drug store's daily cash receipts.

It is hard to believe that as a child I had so little contact with or knowledge of colored people in general since the 1940 census stated that fifty two thousand of them were living in Indianapolis at the time which was 14% of the population. Perhaps the lack of concern and attention to the colored problem was partly because of the widespread impact of the Great Depression and later the focus on winning World War II.

Many white people were in difficult economic straits during the Depression. I remember seeing those tiny tar paper shanties clustered along the banks of White River just south of where Westfield Boulevard crossed the river in Broad Ripple. My parents told me that it wasn't a Hobo Jungle but rather where poor white families lived. I was also told that those hovels had dirt floors and no running water or central heat. As far as the scarcity of food was concerned, I remember seeing destitute white people foraging at Pedigo's Grocery Store refuse bins across the alley from our house. They sifted through the garbage looking for something to eat such as overripe fruits and vegetables.

Mary Ellen and I never saw the connection between the poor and disadvantaged and ourselves when we also rummaged through Pedigo's refuse bin. To us it was a source of many empty wooden orange, lemon, and grapefruit crates, which we carried across the alley to our back yard. With the help of some older children, we dismantled the crates and turned them into fun objects like children's chairs and tables, pushcart bodies, and Kool-Aid stands. Since it was the middle of the Depression and money was scarce, we had few store-bought toys. In those days our parents purchased what was needed, not what we wanted. Consequently we boys and girls spent our spare time engaged in hobbies which required very little hard earned cash, such as collecting common postage stamps and other paper items to paste in our albums and scrapbooks.

Even during the lean Depression years, there was a self-imposed dress code for women. No self-respecting woman went to a tea party, club meeting, church function or department store without wearing her best hat and white gloves even if she couldn't really afford it. No women wore slacks in the 1930s and early 1940s. It wasn't until World War II that women started wearing slacks and then only while working in war production plants where it was practical.

Office workers such as my father usually wore a "uniform" consisting of a double-breasted, pin striped, dark suit, matching vest, suspenders, long sleeved white shirt, colorful tie, felt or straw hat depending on the season, and polished dress shoes. When Dad arrived home from work, the first thing he did was change into his leisure clothes, an older double-breasted suit. He also removed his vest and tie and sometimes exchanged his dress shoes for slippers.

In those days men as well as women wore hats. I can still remember Dad coming home from the office on a spring day and stating that he had seen a man on a downtown street walk up to a stranger, grab his fedora off his head and sail it away. It turns out that on May 15th each year, all self-respecting men were "required" to change their hats from winter felts to summer straws. If they forgot to change hats they were subject to the prank described above.

In the 1930s and 1940s some businessmen like my father also wore spats, garters and suspenders. Pocket watches were still popular, and the suit vest was ready made for them and the small gold plated penknife that Dad carried. These two items of men's jewelry were attached to opposite ends of a gold watch chain that was suspended between two opposing vest pockets. Cloth spats were worn only on cold winter days, their purpose being to keep the ankles warm. The spats buttoned around the ankle between the lower leg and upper foot. Men's garters were used to keep up their three-quarter length hose. Men's suspenders were popular because they were not as confining as belts and one size fit all. Just to play it safe, some of the more conservative men wore suspenders and a belt.

WARTIME ON THE HOME FRONT

The entry of the United States into World War II in late 1941 was felt in the Indiana heartland. As a ten-year old I was well aware of the war effort and battles being fought overseas. However, unlike most of my classmates, I didn't know anyone personally who served in the military during the war. Dad had served in World War I, as had both of his brothers. My cousins were too young to serve, and I didn't know any young men in our neighborhood of the right age to be in the military. During the war, the daily newspaper had war maps showing the location of opposing armies and who was winning or losing the battles. We cut out the maps and pasted them in our scrapbooks. We also read and saved all of the articles written by war correspondent Ernie Pyle of Dana, Indiana, who was reporting from the fields of battle in Africa, Europe and later the Pacific. He didn't report the war from an easy chair in London as other war correspondents did. We were shocked to read in the April 19, 1945, edition of the local newspaper that Ernie had been killed in action the previous day on Ie Shima, a small island near Okinawa, by a Japanese machine gunner.

During World War II American soldiers left their calling card wherever they were stationed in the world. Their card was a simple line drawing of a figure peeking over a fence or wall inscribed with the phrase "Kilroy Was Here." It seemed that wherever there was a flat surface, a serviceman drew the cartoon character Kilroy. He was always pictured having a very large nose, very small, beady eyes and was usually bald. This art form quickly made its way back to the states where it spread rapidly perhaps because drawing Kilroy required no artistic talent whatsoever. All of us kids decorated our school notebooks, textbooks and whatever else was at hand with the Kilroy figure in endless permutations. Like so many other fads the thrill of drawing Kilroy was gone in a few weeks and we looked to other diversions from the tedious chore of book learning. However, Kilroy remains a permanent American icon and is etched on a granite panel on the National World War II Memorial in Washington D.C.

In school, we studied the war and purchased war bond stamps. For us the choice was either the ten-cent red or the twenty-five-cent green savings stamp, which we pasted in small booklets. When the booklets were filled, we exchanged them at the bank for a $25.00 war savings bond that required $18.75 in stamp face value. Another home front activity was the victory vegetable garden. Dad and several neighbors were able to obtain a small plot of ground in a vacant lot at 5500 North Meridian Street, where the Meridian Street Methodist church now stands. Although our yield of radishes, tomatoes, green peppers and beans was small, we felt that we were helping the war effort.

As a Cub Scout and later a Boy Scout during the war, my most energetic effort was rounding up scrap metal such as pots and pans which could be later melted down and made into war implements. We Scouts pulled wagons around the neighborhood, begging for old metal stuff. First we soaked all the labels off the fruit and vegetable cans that we collected and then flattened them for transport to the nearest scrap metal depot. For the war effort, I also collected tin foil from discarded gum and candy wrappers and Dad's empty cigarette packs. In the Boy Scouts we had war bond drives. Every Scout who could bring in a minimum amount of war bond pledges was awarded a special merit badge. Another activity was rounding up used fats and lard for the war effort. We took them to our local butcher who gave us a few cents per pound for our efforts.

Every few weeks we had a blackout test. At the sound of the neighborhood air raid sirens, all exterior and interior lights had to be extinguished. The streets quickly became silent—no automobiles, no streetlights, no traffic lights, no neon signs, and no pedestrians on the sidewalks. It was as quiet and dark as the inside of a tomb. Even home radios were turned off as we crouched down in our damp, dark basement waiting for the all clear siren. The block air raid warden had to check every house in the neighborhood for any sign of light. Woe unto the homeowner who didn't remember to turn off a light somewhere in the house.

Every family with a car was affected by gasoline rationing. Automobiles were required to have a gas ration decal displayed on the front windshield. Since Dad rode the streetcar to and from work he was only entitled to an "A" stamp and ration book, which afforded him the smallest allotment of gasoline. A doctor for example was awarded the more liberal "C" gas ration decal because of his need to visit hospitals and make house calls. In addition, every car had to display a Federal Use Tax Stamp on the windshield. The money raised in this way benefited the war effort. There were also ration stamps for meat, sugar, coffee, flour and butter. Certain days of the week were specified as meatless or wheatless days, during which we were to forgo those rationed items.

As a way of showing his patriotism during WW II, Dad proudly displayed a decal in his rear car window that said "Keep it under 40—Drive for Victory." He did his very best to avoid driving over forty miles an hour even out on the main highways and rural roads.

This wartime decal was the only one he thought suitable to display on his 1933 Buick. I had traded some comic books for travel decals from other states and thought they would look impressive in the rear window of our car but Dad said no. We had some neighbors who displayed so many travel decals in their car rear windows that they had to rely on side mirrors for a look behind.

TORNADOES, FIRES, FLOODS, DISEASE AND OTHER DISASTERS

In addition to the economic deprivation caused by the Great Depression and World War II, there were also natural disasters in the form of high water, strong winds, fires, and disease. In the late 1930s Indianapolis had a mini-tornado that touched down on the north side of town near our house. One casualty of the high winds was a small manufacturing building located a couple of blocks east of the Monon railroad tracks on 54th Street. As soon as I heard about the damage I rode my bike over to get a closer view. It looked as if the roof of the building had been lifted off by a giant and laid gently on the ground several feet away. I was very disappointed, because there wasn't much other evidence of the storm's destruction. However, my disappointment soon turned to joy. On the way home I noticed a small trash heap not far from the railroad tracks. Although we boys had spent a great deal of time walking along the tracks in the past, we had not paid any attention to the trash heap before. This time, several envelopes sticking out of the castoff junk caught my eye. Someone had thrown away several old letters dating back to the 1880s and 1890s with neat old postage stamps. I scooped them up; for me, an inveterate stamp collector, this was a real find.

The year 1937 was known as the Year of the Great Flood. By February of that year the Ohio, Wabash, and White Rivers were all well above their flood stages. The hardest hit cities were those bordering the Ohio River in southern Indiana, including Evansville, New Albany, Jeffersonville, and Aurora. In Indianapolis, it was feared that the White River might overflow its banks and flood the surrounding areas, particularly the Broad Ripple area, as had happened during the 1913 Flood. The most vulnerable local communities were on the north side since Ravenswood, Rocky Ripple and Warfleigh were all prone to flooding. After the 1913 flood, the U.S. Corps of Engineers reinforced the local White River levees to prevent future flooding, but it still happened. Our family drove over to Rocky Ripple to see if there was any damage. Dad later donated several Navy blankets to the flood victims, blankets which he had brought home from his service in World War I. Dad had served on the smallest ship in the Navy at the time, the sub-chaser, patrolling the Mediterranean Sea. The sub-chaser also had the distinction of being the only ship in the Navy that was still wood hulled.

There were several house fires in our neighborhood in those days because coal and wood were the two fuels available for home heating. It was not uncommon for chimney flues to catch on fire because of soot which had collected there over time. By the time the fire engines from the Broad Ripple station arrived with sirens blaring, a crowd of kids had collected from a wide area to watch the action. Fortunately most of the fire damage to houses was confined to roof areas near the chimneys.

IT'S A BIRD! IT'S A PLANE!

On a happier note for boys and girls in the 1930s and the 1940s life was all about airplanes. In the 1930s the newspapers were filled with articles about flying exploits, speed records, and new airplane designs, but the news was not always good. In 1935 the headlines shouted that humorist Will Rogers and Wiley Post were killed in an Arctic airplane crash, while the 1937 newspapers were filled with stories about the zeppelin Hindenburg crash at Lakehurst, New Jersey, with the loss of several passengers and crew members. On a lighter note, one of our favorite Sunday comic strips was *Smilin' Jack*, that dashing pilot, and his side kick, Fat Stuff, who flew off to one after another madcap adventure. At the Uptown movie theater the weekly Pathé news reels filled us in on the latest airplane happenings. At home we boys read about flying adventures in those colorful dust jacketed books such as *Dave Dawson in the Dawn Patrol* series, *the Airplane Boys,* and *The Flying Machine Boys.* Every weekday afternoon we listened to radio serials such as "*Captain Midnight and his Secret*

Squadron" with that church bell striking twelve midnight in the background, *Hop Harrigan, "America's Ace of the Airways"* with his famous opening line "CX-4 calling Control Tower" and *Sky King, "America's Favorite Flying Cowboy."*

If that wasn't enough about flying in our young lives, the family joined in playing board and card games such as Ski-Hi, Flying the Beam, and Wings, to name a few. It is no wonder that a popular hobby for boys then was to build rubber band powered balsa wood airplanes from model kits. All we supposedly needed was the ability to read the instructions, a tube of wood glue, an X-Acto knife and some skill working with very small pieces of balsa wood, colored tissue paper and decals. Unfortunately I was not too adept at doing same and as a consequence my room was strewn with the skeletons of partially completed airplanes. Fortunately I did know how to make simple folded paper airplanes which were sometimes launched from the back row of a PS 84 class room during a particularly boring session on verb tenses.

As an avid collector of just about everything paper, I had my share of Bond Bread match book covers featuring a series of Navy fighting planes. I also collected Piper Cub match book covers which advertised that you could buy a Piper Cub airplane for "as little as $333 down and easy monthly installments." The inside match cover advertised that "a Piper Cub wing lapel emblem could be acquired by sending in just ten cents in stamps or coin." At the same time Wing cigarettes issued a series of fifty small trading cards, one of which was included in every Wings cigarette pack. Each trading card pictured an airplane in color along with a description of the airplane's features.

A 1930s school survey revealed that airplane pilot was the number one choice of young boys as an occupation followed by policeman and doctor. Girls chose nursing as their first choice for a career followed by teaching. Girls had a chance to fly as well since on-board nurses were part of the flight crew in those early days of flying.

By the start of World War II we boys knew our airplanes, both friendly and enemy, and were ready to spot the appearance of any enemy aircraft foolish enough to venture into our airspace. As a Cub Scout I patrolled my small back yard keeping a careful watch for the first sound of an approaching airplane. I scanned the sky with Dad's old German binoculars which he had "borrowed" from a dead enemy combatant during WW I. When I spotted an airplane I pulled out my official airplane spotter guide which had silhouette pictures of all of the enemy warplanes we might sight. The pictures ranged from the likeness of the Japanese Zero to the German Messerschmitt 109. If we spotted a suspicious airplane, we were to report to the nearest block air raid warden. While on backyard patrol we boys felt akin to the official military and civilian air plane spotters active along our coasts during World War II. Although I never spotted an enemy aircraft, I did see some interesting sights including some scantily clad young ladies sunbathing in a neighbor's back yard.

During that period books about flying were not just for boys. In the 1930s, girls read the *Vicki Barr—Flight Stewardess* series of books and the *Ruth Darrow* flying stories. Girls had their real live flying heroines as well such as Anne Morrow Lindbergh who accompanied her husband, Lucky Lindy, on many of his flights. Anne Morrow was known as the First Lady of the Air. Perhaps the best known woman flyer then was Amelia Earhart. She was the holder of many flight records including the first woman to fly solo across the Atlantic in 1932 and she was the holder of many speed records. Amelia also was a participant in the first transcontinental air race in 1929 known as the Powder Puff Derby open only to women. While a faculty member at Purdue University in 1937, Amelia set out on a flight to encircle the globe. Unfortunately Amelia and her navigator Fred Noonan were lost at sea en route to Howland Island in the Pacific Ocean never to be heard from again.

With all of the airplane talk it wasn't a surprise when Mary Ellen asked for an airplane ride as her 12th birthday present in 1941. The flight was to depart from the Indianapolis Weir Cook airport at the Roscoe Turner Terminal. Colonel Roscoe Turner was a flamboyant aviator and promoter who had gained fame as a WW I pilot. His picture appeared frequently in newspapers and magazines of the period. In 1929, he had formed Nevada Airlines, which lasted only a few months due to the Great Depression. That same year he started flying in competitive air races. Over the next ten years he won many transcontinental air races and he was the only person to win the famous Thompson speed race three times. In 1939 Turner moved his opera-

tions to the Weir Cook airport. The Turner enterprise was primarily a
school for pilots, mechanics, and control tower operators. In 1947 he
started Turner Airlines which became part of Lake Central Airlines
in 1950.

ROSCOE TURNER AT WEIR COOK AIRPORT

My family drove out to the airport with great anticipation. None
of us had ever been to any airport before, much less ridden on an
airplane. The small single-engine Turner plane taxied to the pickup
point, where Mary Ellen and Dad were anxiously waiting to board.
Mom and I watched with fascination as the little plane taxied slowly
down the runway and finally struggled into the air. It soon disappeared
from view as the plane headed towards downtown. A few minutes
later it reappeared in the sky and landed safely. It was all over but the
memories. Sure enough, the next month when my birthday was only a
few days away, I was also given the chance to ride in the same airplane
or receive the cash equivalent. But I had enough of a thrill watching
Mary Ellen fly and I opted for the money. In those days ten dollars in
cold cash was like a king's ransom to a kid of ten. It wasn't too many

years later that I had my first ride in a large transport plane while serving in the US Army. However, it was to be another fifty-five years before I rode as a nervous passenger in a small, single engine airplane that resembled the Turner airplane.

THE TUCKER TORPEDO

As teenagers our interest in cars intensified as some of our country's manufacturing giants went back to producing automobiles at the end of World War II in 1945. All of the former car manufacturers retooled their production lines to gear up for new models. In addition to the big three domestic car makers, there were several independents including Hudson, Kaiser, Frazier, Nash, Studebaker, Crosley, Willys and that car of all cars, the Tucker.

The most revolutionary of the new automobiles was the rear engine Tucker. The car was the brain child of Preston Tucker, part-time engineer and full-time sales promoter. Tucker had spent many years hanging out at the Indianapolis Motor Speedway in the1930s and 1940s. In the middle thirties he partnered on building several racecars with Henry Ford. Tucker lived in a mansion in William's Creek on the north side of the city and later moved to a twenty-acre farm just northwest of Noblesville on SR 38. By 1936 he was president and general manager of the Indianapolis Packard sales operation. With his clout he was able to have the Packard named as the 1938 Indy 500 pace car.

PRESTON TUCKER AT INDIANAPOLIS
MOTOR SPEEDWAY-1937

By 1946 he was ready to run his own racecar at the Indy 500. It was known as the Tucker Torpedo. Unfortunately the Tucker racecar conked out after twenty-seven laps due to a mechanical problem. He entered two racecars the next year, neither of which finished the race. By that time Tucker was ready to promote his own passenger car which had undergone several rigorous time and endurance trials at the Indianapolis Motor Speedway. Introduced in 1948, the Tucker had several revolutionary features, including a rear mounted engine, a padded dashboard, automatic steering, and a third headlight located in the center of the grille. The third headlight supposedly moved in tandem with the front wheels as they turned. I remember seeing the Tucker on display at the Johnny Williams' Auto Agency at 1219 N. Meridian Street. That section of North Meridian Street was called Automobile Row.

One of the Tucker cars seen around town had a sign in the rear window. "You have just been passed by a Tucker!" The October 1948 promotional piece in a local newspaper stated that over fifty Tucker dealers from the Indianapolis area previewed the car. Unfortunately only a total of fifty three Tucker automobiles were ever manufactured. The Tucker automobile must have had something going for it, because forty-five of those cars are still road worthy today.

LUSTRON—THE HOUSE OF STEEL

At the end of World War II there was a great pent-up demand for housing both by returning veterans and newly weds. To fill this need many radically designed houses were constructed including an all steel house known as the Lustron. This unique house was conceived and developed by a part-time engineer and full-time sales promoter by the name of Carl Strandlund. After obtaining a multi-million dollar loan from the U.S. Government, Strandlund established his house manufacturing operation in a large war surplus factory in Columbus, Ohio. Over a two and one-half year period he was able to produce approximately twenty five hundred porcelain-enameled steel houses.

Part of Strandlund's sales promotion effort was having model Lustron houses erected in major eastern and mid-western cities. In 1948 the Indiana State Fair featured such a model house. The local Lustron dealer-builder was Tom Joyce, the Indianapolis 7-UP bottler. Tom Joyce was the uncle of Richard Joyce, a classmate of mine at PS 84 and later Shortridge High School. Both of Richard's parents were involved with the Lustron operation. His mother was stationed at the Fairgrounds model house to greet prospective buyers while his father later supervised the construction of Lustron houses locally. Some thirty-five Lustron houses were built in Indianapolis over the next one and one-half years, with approximately one hundred and sixty Lustrons constructed throughout the state. The Broad Ripple area had the highest concentration of Lustrons in the city, with eight erected primarily in the Wharfliegh area near the White River and College Avenue.

To the casual observer, the Lustron house with its porcelain steel exterior panels resembled a typical service station of the 1940s. However, a look inside the house revealed several unique design features including ceiling radiant heat, built-in furniture, interior pocket doors, and a combination dishwasher and clothes washer. The Lustron was promoted as termite and rot proof and very low maintenance as it never needed to be painted inside or out. The porcelain clad house exterior could be washed and waxed just like an automobile. Like the Tucker Corporation, a series of lawsuits put the Lustron Corporation out of business in its infancy in 1950. Due to their architectural uniqueness several Lustron houses have been accepted for listing on the National Register of Historic Place in recent years including one which I owned in Indianapolis.

INDIANAPOLIS LUSTRON HOUSE ON NATIONAL REGISTER

SPORTS OF ALL SORTS

By the 1930s, roller-skating had become a popular recreation with teenagers. Every town of any size in Indiana had its own roller rink and skating club with a distinctive logo patch and a decal which was displayed in the rear window of the family car and on the skater's skate case. Collecting decals from other roller rinks became a popular hobby for many teenagers, with much trading involved. Two popular skating rinks in Indianapolis were at Riverside Park on West 30th Street and the Rollerland Skating Rink at 926 N. Pennsylvania Street.

The adult version of roller-skating known as the Roller Derby was also popular with a substantial segment of the local population in the 1930s and 1940s. The Roller Derby first appeared at the State Fairgrounds Coliseum in 1937 and later at the Butler Fieldhouse. The first Roller Derby was so popular that several local theater owners protested, stating that their attendance was down twenty-five percent during Derby meets. The sport was a spin-off of the six-day bicycle races of the Great Depression and was initially an endurance contest among male and female roller skating couples not unlike the dance marathons of the 1930s. The goal of each couple was to complete a distance equivalent to a trip between New York and Los Angeles, on an oval banked indoor track over a four-week period. Later the concept of physical contact and a simple point system were introduced into the game. Here two teams of five skaters whiped around the track bunched together. Each team had a "jammer" who started in the back of the pack and earned points by lapping members of the other team. As with other sports, there were many Roller Derby stars with rabid and loyal fans.

Professional wrestling was another second-tier sport that was popular in Indianapolis during the late 1930s and beyond. Most of the wrestling events were held at the Tyndall Armory at 711 North Pennsylvania Street during the winter months and at the open-air Sports Arena Garden at 521 North Pennsylvania Street in the summer. This block on Pennsylvania Street is now home to the Minton-Capehart Federal Building. I remember seeing Killer Kowalski wrestle at the Armory and Dick Levin, known as the Jewish Heavyweight Champion, wrestle at the outdoor arena. Some of my other favorite wrestlers were Wild Red Berry, Lou Thez, Man Mountain Dean, and Indian Chief Jules Strongbow. As a kid I was amazed how many professional wrestlers seem to come from the titled nobility. There was Baron Michele Leone, Count Billy Varga, Duke Keomuka and Lord James Blears to name a few.

In those days wrestling was more of a legitimate sport and less a theater of the absurd than it is today. No doubt in the 1930s and 1940s, as today, the winner was determined by the promoters in advance of the match. Then, however, the wrestlers relied more on authentic wrestling holds such as those used in international Olympic matches. The aura of wrestling showmanship commenced with the advent of televised matches in the 1950s with such stars as Gorgeous George and Dick "the Bruiser" Afflis.

Dick Afflis whose first name was really William attended Shortridge High School in 1944-1945 and played on the football team. During the summer months he was often seen at the Riveria Club where he amazed us guys with his physical prowess which included doing effortless one-arm pushups. Rumor had it that Bill's favorite sport was fisticuffs not football. After high school was over for the day he walked to the nearby neighborhood tavern at 34th & Illinois Street and waited patiently outside the front door until an unsuspecting bar patron appeared. Afflis then blocked the stranger's path and called him names hoping to end up in a fist fight.

Apparently Afflis continued to engage in this form of extracurricular recreation for the rest of his life. Unfortunately for the Shortridge high school football team and fortunately for the tavern patrons, Afflis left school at the end of his sophomore year and moved to Lafayette, IN where he graduated from Lafayette Jefferson High school in 1947. After a couple of years at Purdue University and then the University of Nevada-Reno, Alfflis had a stint with the Green Bay Packers as a very offensive lineman. In 1955 he found his true calling, beating people up legally, which is known as professional wrestling.

Early in his wrestling career Afflis became known as "Dick the Bruiser." He soon realized that all of the big money in wrestling was going to the promoters and not to the wrestlers. After returning to Indianapolis in the early 1960s, the Bruiser and another heavyweight wrestler, Wilbur Snyder, purchased the rights to the Indianapolis territory of the National Wrestling Alliance (NWA) and renamed it the World Wrestling Association (WWA). As promoter it was a fairly easy task for the Bruiser to become the champion of the association. During his long wrestling career the Bruiser teamed up with another behemoth, The Crusher, and together they won several tag team world championships. The Bruiser was known as the world's most dangerous wrestler.

DICK 'THE BRUISER" READY FOR BATTLE

When the Bruiser was not wrestling, he spent most of his time at his cocktail bar, the Harem Longue, located in the 2200 block of North Meridian Street. He also did charitable works in and around Indianapolis. Fittingly he was lifting weights when he died unexpectedly at the age of sixty two. He died just three weeks after he had won a wrestling match in southern Indiana.

Until we were in high school, the only major sports we listened to on the radio were boxing and baseball. We knew all of the baseball players' names, the positions they played, and their batting averages. Fortunately, it was easier then to keep all those statistics straight in our heads, since there were so few major league baseball teams. For example, we all knew that Pee Wee Reese played short stop and third base for the Brooklyn Dodgers, that his life time batting average at the time was 270 and that he had 885 runs-batted-in. We knew that

Bob Feller (Rapid Robert) of the Cleveland Indians was the fastest pitcher of his day, that he had an earned run average of 3.60, and that he won twenty-seven games in 1940. We knew that Phil "Scooter" Rizzuto of the New York Yankees was a great short stop and had a batting average of 270. We did go to Victory Field, (later renamed Bush Stadium) located on west 16th Street, from time to time to watch the minor league Indianapolis Indians play, but it wasn't the same. The big leagues were where the action was. To listen to the baseball games on radio, we gathered at Warren Rich's house. He had a large floor-model console radio that was positioned just right to sit around and listen to the games. The radio sports commentators were so skilled in those days that they made us feel like we were actually seeing the games in person.

No discussion of professional baseball is complete without mentioning Eddie Feigner, the king of softball pitchers. Eddy's pitching exploits are legendary, covering a playing span of over fifty years. Eddie started pitching semi-pro softball in 1946, after playing the game while serving in the Marine Corps during WW II. He was such a great pitcher that he fielded a team of only four players. They played some of the best fully manned softball teams in countries ranging from the Panama Canal Zone to Pakistan. During the reign of "The King and His Court" as he was billed, he pitched in 7,100 games, of which his abbreviated team won 5,900 games. He often pitched blindfolded, and he struck out over 4,300 players in that manner during his long pitching career. As far as fast balls are concerned, pitcher Bob Feller's fastest overhand pitch was timed at 96.8 miles per hour, while Eddy's fastest underhand pitch was clocked at 104 miles per hour. Many years later I had a chance to watch him pitch at the softball stadium on north Sherman Drive. Although he could barely walk due to arthritis, his pitching arm was still intimidating.

As we boys approached the teen years, our favorite outdoor winter sports were sledding and ice-skating. Every winter the city workers blocked off the long steep hill on Capitol Avenue between 54th and 56th streets after heavy snows. We could sled in the street on our Western Flyers without fear of being hit by a car. This was great fun, since hills in Indianapolis have always been in short supply.

Our family's choice for ice-skating was the pond at the Indiana School for the Blind at 7700 North College Ave. When the ice was thick enough for skating, Dad drove our family there for an outing. Yes, we could have skated at the Indianapolis Coliseum at the State Fairgrounds for a fee, but skating at the Blind School pond was more fun and free. Dad was quite skilled at the sport. The pair of old strap-on ice skates he used was purchased in Holland while he served there in the Navy in World War I. After a few trial runs with his old skates he put on his shoe skates for a little fancy stuff. Those skates had blades that were perfect for figure eight's and other fancy footwork that he skillfully performed on the ice.

Mary Ellen was also pretty good at ice skating which she attributed to her Sonia Henie skates. By the age of fourteen Sonia had become the national champion skater in her native Norway. Three years later she won the world crown, followed by three Olympic ice skating titles. Sonia turned to acting in movies in the 1930s and her most famous movie was *Sun Valley Serenade* in 1941. She also toured the country with her Hollywood Ice Review and appeared frequently at the Indianapolis Coliseum starting with its grand opening in 1939. Since frequent spills led me to spend more time sitting on the ice than on my feet skating, I decided to look elsewhere for fun and excitement much to Dad's disappointment.

Not being much of an athlete, my favorite indoor sport was ping-pong, more accurately called table tennis. Several of my friends had basement ping-pong tables including neighbor Jack Freese, whose father had been state ping-pong champion of New Jersey. Jack's father had also toured the country as a trick shot artist. We were impressed with his collection of sandpaper faced paddles of all sizes and shapes, including one in the shape of a question mark. One time Jack's father challenged any of us to play a game of ping-pong with him. I took the challenge when Jack's father agreed to use a small china plate instead of a ping-pong paddle. After spotting me a fifteen-point handicap, Jack's father won the game twenty-one to sixteen.

My interest in ping-pong was influenced in the1940s by the publicity surrounding Jimmy McClure, a 1931 Shortridge High School graduate at the age of fifteen. Jimmy was well suited to the non-contact sport of ping-pong at barely five feet tall and a weight of 125 pounds.

While in high school he won the Indianapolis City and Indiana State open table tennis championships. At Shortridge he played tennis and danced in several school performances. After graduation from high school, Jimmy became a tap dancer with the traveling Texas Guinan dance troupe. Texas Guinan was a former movie actress and nightclub entertainer with an unsavory reputation who had a traveling dance revue. After her untimely death in 1933, Jimmy returned to Indianapolis to resume his ping-pong career. Two years later he played against the world champion Victor Barna in London, as reported in the February 1935 issue of *Time Magazine*. Over a period of years he became national singles champion five times and doubles champion several times. After retirement from competitive play, he operated a retail sporting goods store on the near north side of Indianapolis and had his own line of personalized Jimmy McClure ping-pong paddles.

When some of us older teenage boys were at that awkward age of all arms, legs and mouth, we started to worry about our scrawny physiques. We were tired of seeing ourselves as the before poster boy for the muscle builder ads in the comic books. In the 1940s body builders George Jowett "World's Greatest Body Builder" and Charles Atlas "The World's Most Perfectly Developed Man" duked it out in ads in comic books and men's magazines. Charles Atlas promised to make you a new man with dynamic tension while Jowett's ads promised to make you tough as a Marine with dynamic muscles. The idea was for the reader to send away for the necessary muscle building instruction booklets ranging in price from twenty-five cents to one dollar. The popular Charles Atlas cartoon ad showed a 110-pound weakling on the beach sunbathing, when suddenly a bully came up and kicked sand in his face. Every week that same guy had sand kicked in his face until one day he sent in his money for the Charles Atlas course. The rest is history. After a few short weeks of dynamic tension, the weakling became a mass of muscles. At the next meeting on the beach, of course he knocked the bully out.

I went for the Atlas program since their ads were more colorful than Jowett's, and I really liked the ad about the bully and the skinny guy at the beach. I worked out with the dynamic tension system for a while and did indeed show some change in my physical stature. In six months I went from a 135-pound weakling to a 140-pound weakling.

Incidentally, I imagine that the name Charles Atlas was more marketable than his real name, Angelo Siciliano.

Believing that the only real way to get muscles was to work out in a gym, a few of us high school seniors enrolled in a weight lifting program at the Indianapolis Barbell Studio on Massachusetts Avenue, east of College Avenue. I often saw Bobby, the manager of the gym, driving around town in his miniature 1948 Crosley station wagon. It had fake wood paneling on its metal doors. In those days many real wood-bodied station wagons had the name of a lodge, camp, ranch or other type of resort painted on their doors. Bobby had the name "Got No Rancho" painted on his station wagon doors.

After we had been at the gym a few weeks, we noticed a very muscular young man named Miklos Hargitay. He was a recent refugee from Hungry who was employed in Indianapolis as a hod carrier and later as an adagio dancer. As time went on he spent more hours in the gym building his body and less working for a living. We followed his career throughout the state in body building competitions and we were present when he won the Mr. Tri-State contest in Muncie in the late 1940s. He was the Arnold Schwarznegger of his day. I lost track of him early in his body building career when I stopped going to the gym. Nothing was happening to my body there.

Twenty years later when living in Los Angeles, I saw a convertible with the top down pull out of a Sunset Boulevard driveway that wound back to a huge pink mansion. The driver looked familiar, and yes it was Miklos, or Mickey as he called himself. With a little research I found out the Beverly Hills house belonged to Mickey and actress Jayne Mansfield, his wife. Apparently she spied Mickey in a line up of beefcake in the Mae West Revue, a 1950s Las Vegas stage show. Within two years they were married and starred together in some forgettable grade B movies in the 1960s. He had come a long way from that dark, dismal gym in downtown Indianapolis.

LIFE IN THE UNDERWORLD

During the 1930s the overall crime rate throughout the country was surprisingly low given the state of the economy. However, organized gangs of crooks did roam the country pulling bank heists, armored car holdups, business payroll robberies, jewelry and fur store burglaries, and every now and then just for a change of pace, a kidnapping or two. Traffic in prostitution, illegal drugs and liquor was left to the Mafia to handle. Hoosier gangs consisted of younger, white, Anglo-Saxon males mainly from small Indiana towns and farms; no foreign born Mafia types here. Perhaps the best known Indiana criminals who terrorized the Midwest during the Depression were in the Dillinger gang headed up by that Mooresville farm boy, John Dillinger. Another famous Hoosier gang was the Brady-Schaffer gang lead by Alfred Brady from Kentland, Indiana. The Brady-Schaffer gang was described by J. Edgar Hoover of the F.B.I. as the most vicious and dangerous gang in history in 1937. In just the prior eighteen months that gang committed one hundred and fifty holdups and two murders. The F.B.I. entered the picture in 1937 when the gang supposedly crossed the state line after a jewelry store robbery.

For us kids our idea of what constituted a gang was based on that popular radio program *Gang Busters* which aired in the late 1930s and through the 1940s. The program grew out of the exploits of Indiana's own John Dillinger. The opening soundtrack was unforgettable—the sharp blast of a policeman's whistle, the shuffling feet of a chain gang, the sound of a window breaking, the shrill noise of an activated burglar alarm, the eerie wail of the police siren, the roar of a Thompson sub-machine gun, and the screech of automobile tires.

In black and white movies of the period called Film Noir, gangsters were portrayed as true professionals, usually dressed to the nines in double breasted pin striped suits with padded shoulders, fancy dress shirts, vests, hand painted ties, wide suspenders, two tone oxfords and felt fedoras. Those gangsters were usually armed with Thompson sub-machine guns and rode around in big, black Packards or LaSalles with those huge side mounted tires. If any of them deigned to pack a rod, it was housed in an attractive, genuine leather holster which was neatly concealed under the arm for easy access and no tell-tale bulges in their double breasted suit coat. Gang members were usually clean shaven and their hair was slicked down with the latest type of hair pomade.

In the movies gang members were often graduates of the Big House or the state pen. My favorite movie star gangsters in those films were George Raft, Humphrey Bogart and James Cagney. Their crime of choice was usually the small town bank job. Those country banks were plentiful, poorly guarded, and get-a-ways were a cinch since the gangs could easily out run the local cops or county sheriffs in their high powered cars, some of which featured armor plate. However, in the real world during the 1930s those small town bank jobs became more difficult to pull off because states such as Indiana organized state police forces for the express purpose of putting the small town bank robbers out of business. Favorite gang hideouts were seedy hotels and flop houses. Most of their time was spent sitting around kibitzing, drinking illegal booze, and playing poker. If one of their bank heists hit it big time the gang holed up in one of those fancy resorts like the French Lick Springs Hotel.

I wonder whatever happened to their colorful language and those wonderful gang nick names like Greasy Thumb Guzik and Mad Dog Vincent Coll. The conversation of a gang member relating the highlights of a recent small town bank job to one of his pals might have gone something like this: "Yah Muscles, it was a slick job. Lefty cased the joint before the caper. Everything looked jake. We had the Professor (the brains of the gang since he was the only gang member to have graduated from high school) draw up the layout of the heist. Four Eyes was the lookout on the job and Shorty was our driver. The guys packing the "Tommies" were Butch and Dutch. As soon as we knocked over that hayseed bank, we scrammed out of that hick berg in the Dusey with the bulls in hot pursuit, but we ditched the flatfoots out on the main drag. We then met our gun molls at Big Al's Roadhouse where we downed a few boilermakers before dividing up the swag which was loaded with C notes. I then split with Gert. That doll is a real looker with a great pair of gams. She likes to flash that two carat sparkler that I gave her as a souvenir from that ice job on her left pinkie. Boy, that rock is worth a lot of clams! Hey Muscles, how about one more shot of rotgut before we take it on the lam?"

In addition to real and pretend gang mayhem and murder, I enjoyed reading about the type of crime found in the private detective genre books of Raymond Chandler, Dashiell Hammet, and Mickey Spillane. Those authors wrote about hard boiled, big boozing, gum shoes like Phillip Marlowe, Sam Spade, and Mike Hammer as they roamed the streets of big cities like New York and Los Angeles while working on a case. Often those private eyes were on the lookout for the archetypical stoolie that was just out of the slammer and would fink on a brother rat for a sawbuck.

Fortunately for Indianapolis most of its crime during the depression wasn't the violent type such as committed by Indiana's own John Dillinger, but took the form of illegal gambling. Then gambling was undertaken as a private enterprise rather than as a sanctioned governmental venture such as the current State lotteries. A September, 1930 Indianapolis Star headline in large, bold type screamed out "Police arrest 80 in drive on lawlessness—Ten quick raids made after indictments in ranks." The next day the headline blared that the "Police raid nine more places in vice war." In those days illegal gambling took many forms including poker and other card games, off track betting on horses, and the numbers racquet. The numbers racquet was perhaps the most widespread and lucrative business for the private entrepreneurs of the day.

The numbers game dates back to the 1500s in Italy and made its appearance in the U.S. prior to the Civil War. The poor were attracted to the game since small amounts of money could be bet. Unlike present day state lotteries, bookies often extended credit to the players. A payoff to winners of at least 600 to one was typical. The idea was for the player to select any set of three numbers to bet on which were written down on what were called bank clearing slips. Those slips in turn were picked up daily by a runner who would hand them over to the local "banker." If the banker couldn't handle all of the daily receipts, a part of the take was laid off to a higher level banker. The difference between the net take and the payoff was called the vigorish which usually ended up in the pocket of the mob boss. The source of the daily winning number combinations ranged from the last three digits of the total bets at a selected racetrack to published Dow Jones stock market numbers.

During the Great Depression, Indianapolis had its own numbers bosses, the Mitchell brothers who operated a variety of gambling dens from the 1930s into the 1970s. The colorful and likeable Mitchell boys were Joseph and his younger brother Isaac, known as Tuffy. They got their start in life as Josef and Isaac Mutchnek in Russia and immigrated to the United States in the early 1920s. Tuffy got his moniker when as a youngster he had more than 100 bouts as a flyweight boxer. The brothers operated billiard parlors, cafes, taverns, liquor stores and night clubs on and around Indiana Avenue in the heart of the colored club area. The boys' night clubs included the Cotton Club, the Pink Poodle, the Mitchelynn, and The Palms Club-Hotel.

Many of Indy's colored jazz musician notables such as Jimmy Coe got their start in one of the Mitchell clubs at a time when there was open segregation. Tuffy once described himself as "the king of Indiana Avenue." It was said at the time that he had a lot of friends in blue uniforms. Whenever an officer had a personal problem, Tuffy was always good for money or gifts. Perhaps Tuffy was too generous with the men in blue. In 1964 twenty two Indianapolis policemen were indicted for accepting bribes from Mitchell to ignore his numbers racquet although ultimately only one policeman went to jail. We always wondered if the brothers were connected to the Syndicate.

More than 100 articles appeared in the local papers on the exploits of the Mitchell brothers over a forty year period beginning with older brother's Joe arrest for keeping a gambling house in 1930. At that time illegal gambling was rampant in Indianapolis. Joe had a few more run-ins with the police over the years but couldn't begin to match his younger brother Tuffy in that category

Although Tuffy continued to make front page news, we were fairly sure that he would never become "Public Enemy Number One." That dubious title was first given to Al Capone by the Chicago Crime Commission in 1930. Tuffy didn't seem to mind having his name in the papers and even had his name put on personal give-a-ways ranging from lead pencils to his likeness on match book covers. I guess that it paid to advertise. Although most of his arrests were for gambling, once he was arrested and later sued by an individual for assault and battery. The "victim" was 6' 2" and weighed 225 pounds while Tuffy was variously described as being somewhere between 5'1" and 5' 6" tall and weighed 130 pounds.

For his court appearances, Tuffy always dressed like the successful businessman that he was. In court Tuffy felt that he was misunderstood. As he said more than once to the judge, "I am a good citizen, a charity worker not a gambler. I am not a criminal. I've tried to be legitimate…had a hamburger stand and ice cream parlor…but I failed. I have given money to the United Hebrew Congregation on the South Side. I am really a charitable man. I purchased a television set for the Jewish Old Age Home, and gave 100 prayer books to my synagogue." Tuffy must have always carried a Monopoly Game "get out of jail free" card since by early 1954, although he had been arrested 40 times, he never spent one full day in jail. Once he was arrested twice in one day. His lack of jail time may also have been due to the number of high powered lawyers he employed as defense counsels. They included a Sam Blum who had formerly been a deputy prosecutor in charge of several cases against Tuffy. Unfortunately Tuffy finally got caught plying his trade once too often and in late 1954 served 78 days of a 90 day sentence in the Indiana State Prison for gambling. It is believed that his gambling operation generated more than $1,000,000 a year in revenues at the time. He finally made the big time in 1964 when the Feds convicted him of failing to pay Federal wagering taxes and he was sentenced to five years in the big house. He was released from prison after a two-year stay and being a good citizen; he immediately applied for and was granted a federal gambling stamp for wagering as reported in the September 13, 1954 issue of *Time* magazine.

TUFFY READY FOR ANOTHER COURT APPEARANCE
Indianapolis Star, photographer Joe Young

Tuffy's exploits continued to make front page news until 1974 when he died of a heart attack while playing pool in a north side dive, The Happy Landings Bar, in Ravenswood. As always Tuffy was true to his calling. He was $700 ahead in bets which he had made over a four hour period at the pool table when he collapsed trying to make the eight ball the hard way. When the investigators searched his car parked outside the bar for possible contraband they found the following items: ten 4-play poker games, four bibles, a two-piece billiard cue, four religious pictures, several "dream" books used by gambling hunch players, a 20 piece set of dinnerware, a package of billiard chalk, 13 liquor dispensers, two radios and a set of false teeth with the name "Tuff" on the back. At the time of his death, Tuffy was free on a $1000 appeal bond from a $300 fine and a 180 day jail sentence. As a former police inspector said of Tuffy after his death, "He was a colorful character. He was from another era." Those in the know today say that Tuffy gave better odds on his gambling games in the old days than the state of Indiana gives on its various lotteries today.

IN THE WORKING WORLD

Life was not all school, holidays, summer vacations, fun and games and movies at the Uptown Theater. My first job outside of the house was at the tender age of ten when I signed up for a neighborhood magazine route. I was given a small white canvas carrying bag and a list of about fifteen existing customers. They all lived within a few blocks of my house, so I could walk the route. Two of my customers lived in a large, imposing apartment building in the 5300 block of College Avenue. I was intimidated at first, as I had never been inside such a large building. The long, dimly lit hallways were not very inviting. However, after a few weeks of delivering *Look, Colliers,* and *Liberty* magazines in the apartment building, I became accustomed to the routine.

In the 1940s, we had three newspapers, the *Indianapolis Star,* the *Indianapolis News* and the *Indianapolis Times.* Many of my eleven to thirteen-year-old classmates delivered one of these newspapers to earn some extra money. I decided against the *Star* because I didn't want to get up at five A.M. every morning in the dark to deliver the paper. I ruled against the *Times* because it had so few subscribers that the routes were very long. So at age twelve, I was hired to deliver the afternoon *News* on a route near School 84. As soon as school let out, I rode my bike to the designated corner where a delivery truck had dropped off the bundles of papers. I folded each paper so it could easily sail through the air from my bike to the customer's porch. I stacked the folded papers in my cloth delivery bag, and either slung it over my shoulder or strapped it to the bicycle handlebars. Since most of the houses in my neighborhood stood just a few feet back from the sidewalk, I seldom needed to get off my bike and walk the paper to the front door, but there were a few fastidious customers who wanted their newspaper in a specific location such as in the paper holder attached to the porch mailbox. Delivering newspapers wasn't much fun when it rained or snowed, and I always had to be on the lookout for roaming dogs and neighborhood bullies.

Every now and then a special edition of the paper was published about a major event. One example was the unexpected death of President Franklin Delano Roosevelt in April 1945. We newsboys received a call from our local paper route supervisor telling us when and where the special edition was to be picked up. We were expected to hawk the special on the designated street corners around Broad Ripple. We jockeyed for a popular corner and tried to be the first newsboy there.

The only excitement I remember while delivering papers was a police raid on one of my customers on Central Avenue. Apparently the homeowner had been operating an off-track betting joint in his basement for some time. Perhaps the fact that the family had several telephone lines was a clue. They must have had some pull or money to obtain more than one telephone line because even having a single one-party line was a rarity.

The one day a month I dreaded most was when I collected money for the paper in person. Too often the customer was not at home or at least didn't answer my knock at the front door. Other times they said I had to come back another day when they had the correct change. Newsboys appreciated the "prepays" who paid the newspaper company in advance; no collection hassle there. Having a paper route was good training for later life, as we learned how to handle money, meet new people, deal with problems, and generally run a business, albeit a very small one.

Besides my early magazine and newspaper routes, I cut grass for several neighbors and later set pins at the Broad Ripple Bowling Alley on Broad Ripple Avenue, which stood near the Monon tracks where the current McDonald's Restaurant is located. One of my jobs as pin setter was lifting the bowling ball back into the track after it was thrown down the alley and giving it a hearty shove toward the front end of the alley. The thing to remember was to jump up on the surrounding back wall of the alley before the ball reached the pins. If not, I could get hit either by the ball or by one of the flying pins. I also had to reset any pins that had been knocked down in the lane placing them into their proper position in the overhead pin rack. Every time a bowler was finished, I reset the ten pins in their proper place by manually lowering the pin rack. If all went well and I kept track of when to reposition the pins during the game, I might receive a tip by the bowler who would throw the coin down the entire length of the alley into my outstretched hands.

During high school, I worked at Merchants National Bank in their downtown headquarters at 11 South Meridian Street. My job was counting and wrapping denominations of coins, which were loose in heavy sealed canvas bags. My wrapping job was done in the lower reaches of the bank basement. I didn't mind the dirty job, the darkness of the room, or the fact that no one else ever ventured down there. What I didn't like was being required to wear a white shirt and tie on the job.

Another high school job was at the I.U. Medical Center bookstore on west Michigan Street. My assignment was to do odd jobs at the direction of the two female co-owners. It was the first but not the last time that a woman other than my mother or a teacher gave me marching orders. My one perk was being allowed to glance at the various medical textbooks when things were quiet. My favorite textbook was *Gray's Anatomy*. It had some very educational pictures.

One summer during high school I worked with a friend Fred Bates at his father's religious publishing firm, Kriebel and Bates, in downtown Indianapolis. The company had the exclusive rights to publish all of the paintings by artist Warner Sallman. During World War II, the U.S. government issued every serviceman and woman a wallet size print of the Head of Christ, Sallman's most famous painting. By 1970 fifty million prints of the artwork had been sold making it the most popular artwork ever painted.

My job that summer at Kriebel and Bates, along with several other friends, was boxing sets of greeting cards called Flowers of the Bible land. The ten different cards were stacked in separate piles around the room. Our job was to grab a different card off each of the ten piles, count out ten envelopes, stuff them in a box, and stack them on a table.

Unfortunately I didn't realize that the table where we had stacked the finished product was a drafting table. I inadvertently leaned on the horizontal tabletop, which quickly became vertical, and the hundreds of stacked boxes spilled onto the floor. We guys hurriedly picked up the scattered cards and envelopes and stuffed them back in the boxes without much care. For several months after that, the company received complaints from customers, such as "The boxes of Flowers of the Bible land cards we received were a real mess. In some cases there were three identical cards with roses, two with lilies and no tulip or crocus cards. Other boxes you sent us had as many as twelve cards and only eight envelopes." I didn't work there again!

The next Christmas holiday I delivered the U.S. mail out of the postal sub-station at 42nd and College Avenue as a temporary worker. Unfortunately I was assigned mail delivery in a very bad neighborhood filled with mean dogs, rusty mailboxes, and few house numbers. I didn't work there again! The next summer I worked for R. L. Polk and Company, publishers of the Indianapolis city directory. My job, along with many other part-timers, was updating the demographic data found on individual household address cards for the assigned area. Once again I was given a bad neighborhood to work. Often when I knocked on the resident's door to see if any changes were needed in the data, no one appeared to be at home. However more times than not, I saw the occupant peer out through a closed curtain or blinds to see who was at the door. I came away with the idea they thought I might be a bill collector. Consequently the going was very slow, and many of the data cards remained unchanged as "no-shows." I didn't work there again!

I had another part-time job as cloak room attendant at the Masonic Temple at 525 North Illinois Street. Every weekend some evening activity was held such as a formal dance or an induction ceremony for men joining one of the Masonic orders. It was a fun job since several of my friends worked there part-time as well. The one admonition from the boss was "don't go through the overcoat pockets looking for loose change." We usually took a break during the event and walked to the nearby White Castle. It was time for some gut bombs. We purchased six hamburgers and a Coke for thirty five cents. As with most small White Castles at that time, it was standing room only with no chairs or booths to sit in. Although I made only fifty cents an hour, I did work at the Masonic Temple again.

My longest tenure at one teenage job was behind the soda fountain at Haag's Drugstore at the corner of 54th and College Avenue. Rhude had worked there for a while so I had someone to teach me the fine art of soda jerking. Our main job was making and serving basic fountain drinks and desserts. We also prepared lunchroom type salads and sandwiches such as hamburgers, hot dogs, grilled cheese, and tenderloins. In addition, we hand dipped a variety of ice cream flavors in those hard-to-fill stiff, white paper pint and quart containers.

I will never forget the time I struck it rich or nearly so while at work. I had just closed up Haag's soda fountain operation for the evening and was doing the usual cleanup chores. After sanding the cooking grill with a pumice stone I started to sweep up around the soda fountain stools. Suddenly I spied something on the floor that looked like folding money. I pounced on it like a dog on a bone. It was a small fortune; a one dollar bill. That amount represented nearly three hours of hard labor. I immediately told the other Haag's employees about my good fortune and was told by the boss that "finder's keepers, loser's weepers." I could hardly wait to get home to tell my family about my good luck.

The next afternoon I was working behind the soda fountain and an older man sat down at the counter. Without any preamble he said, I understand that you found a one dollar bill here last night; that was mine. I was flabbergasted and felt somewhat intimidated because he was an adult. I had never seen him in the drugstore before but I reluctantly reached into my billfold and pulled out the lonely dollar and handed it over to him. Without as much as a thank you or good by he left the drugstore. When I described the incident to my friend Rhude the next day, he replied, "from your description of him that must have been my neighbor, Mr. Temple. Did you know that he won the Broad Ripple American Legion raffle two years running and both times won a new Plymouth?" From the sound of things I needed the dollar more than he did. In retrospect I should have made him give me the bill's serial number before handing it over to him.

That summer in 1946 when Rhude and I weren't working at the drug store, I usually rode my bike over to his house for an afternoon visit. We sat on those springy steel chairs on his front porch idling away the hours drinking Kool-Aid and talking about this and that and watching the world walk by. Our real motive for sitting there was to catch a glimpse of either of the two swell looking dolls who lived in his neighborhood. They often walked by Rhude's house on their way to one of the corner shops. It really made our day if, as one of them walked by, she turned her head, smiled, and said hello.

Back at the drugstore my favorite fountain drink to make was the "suicide" Coke. It was made by combining a squirt of lemon, cherry, vanilla and chocolate flavorings to Coca-Cola fountain syrup and mixing them together in a tall glass with carbonated water. Another favorite drink was the phosphate made by mixing any flavoring with carbonated water and a judicious amount of phosphoric acid to give it that bittersweet aftertaste. The phosphoric acid was so potent that it had to be stored in a small metal shaker and only three or four drops were used in a single fountain drink. I also made fountain Coca-Cola and Pepsi, using the appropriate flavoring and carbonated water. Those creative kids who wanted something a little different purchased a chilled bottle of Royal Crown, Pepsi, or Coke for a nickel and a small bag of Planters Peanuts, and dumped the entire bag of peanuts into the bottle. That way they could "have their Coke and eat 'em too."

All the while I was working behind the soda fountain, there was incessant loud music coming from the store Wurlitzer juke box. After a while it got on my nerves. After all, a kid can only take so many hours of the *Hut-Sut Song* and *Mairzy Doats*. Many years later I learned that the juke box owed its popularity to a gentleman who lived at 54th and Meridian Street, just a few blocks from the drug store. He was Homer E. Capehart, the conservative Republican senator from Indiana, who served in the U.S. Senate from 1945–63 and whose daughter was a friend of my sister Mary Ellen. Prior to that time he had been involved for several years in the early development of the electrically amplified phonograph, better known as the juke box of today. By 1928 Senator Capehart had his own line of juke boxes, the Capehart Orchestrope, which featured several of his technical innovations. In 1932, he left the organization to become general sales manager and vice president for the Rudolph Wurlitzer Manufacturing Company where he promoted the Wurlitzer juke box to the point that it became the generic name for all brands of coin operated record players. It was said that he was the father of the juke box industry who became a multi-millionaire in the process. That wasn't too bad for a farm boy from Algiers, Indiana.

WAS THAT A LEMON-LIME PHOSPHATE?

During my days working at Haag's, I witnessed two memorable events. First was the arrival of the Filipino Twirler Boys. Before the advent of popular television, it was not unusual to have in-store promotions of various items, such as the two young Filipinos performing on the sidewalk to promote Royal Champion yo-yos. The yo-yo's origin is uncertain. A Greek urn from 500 BC shows a youth playing with what is believed to be a yo-yo. By the 16th century, Filipino tribesmen were bonking foes and animals with four-pound yo-yos hurled on twenty-foot cords. The yo-yo arrived in the US in 1867, when a German immigrant named Charles Kirchof began selling his Patented Return Wheel in Newark, NJ, with modest success. Then in the 1920s a young Ohio man named Donald F. Duncan saw a Filipino playing with a yo-yo on a San Francisco dock. Duncan thought that it might be a popular toy with children and started manufacturing yo-yos in 1926. His one improvement spelled success: the Duncan yo-yo used a string with a loop on the end where it slipped over the yo-yo and around its hub. This invention allowed the yo-yo to spin in place at the end of the string until retrieved, which lead to the creation of many different tricks. By 1950 Duncan was selling 30 million yo-yos a year, and their popularity continues today.

The Filipino Twirler Boys were hired by the manufacturers of the Royal Champion yo-yo to take advantage of the market that Duncan had created many years earlier. The boys performed the usual tricks such as Walking the Dog, Around the World, and Cat's Cradle. In addition, they were happy to carve a design on newly purchased Royal Champion yo-yos for the kids. As word spread through the neighborhood, the twirlers soon had a large crowd of youngsters following their every move. Waiting for my chance, I hurried to the store's notions counter and purchased one of the cheaper yo-yos. After all, my forty cents an hour wage didn't go very far. A few years later the minimum wage was raised from forty to seventy five cents per hour when Truman signed The Fair Labor Standards Amendment.

I waited in line to have my new yo-yo carved. Using a common pocketknife, one of the lads carved my very own initials on one side of the yo-yo and the outline of a sailboat, a palm tree and a blazing sun on the other side. I hurried home to try my hand at the tricks I had seen the Filipino boys perform. My first attempt was the *Around the World* trick. Unfortunately my yo-yo stalled out in space soon after it started the journey, and my *Walking the Dog* never got much beyond the first few steps. After several more attempts to master the yo-yo, I reluctantly put it in my bottom bureau drawer. There it rested with other games of skill such as the Wham-O paddle and rubber ball, the ring toss game and the dart gun game, all popular at the time.

The other major happening at Haag's the summer of 1946 was the opportunity to meet the diminutive Johnny of Philip Morris fame in person. With the end of World War II in 1945, cigarette manufacturers began to promote their products again. Gone were the days of cigarette rationing on the home front. I remember in the early forties during WW II, there was a rumor that the drug store was going to receive an allotment of cigarettes. Long lines queued up at the tobacco counter, waiting for sales to begin. Philip Morris had been one of the more popular brands of cigarettes before WW II and hoped to be so after war's end. Several off brands had appeared on the market in the middle 1940s, including one called "Home Run" cigarettes. The pack had a neat picture of an old-time baseball player at bat. The cigarettes must not have been very good, because a popular joke of the day was "if you smoke a Home Run cigarette you will want to run home and get sick." Philip Morris owed part of its success to the popularity of their living trademark, Johnny, who was barely five feet tall. He was always pictured dressed in a crisp red bellhop uniform in ads on billboards, magazines, and later on television. The print ads showed him crying, "Call for Philip Morrrrisss!" This slogan was followed by the statement "stepping out of storefronts all over America to remind smokers that you get no cigarette hangover with Philip Morris."

Johnny's childlike high-pitched voice could also be heard in commercials on the popular radio program, Philip Morris Playhouse. Johnny, whose last name was Roventini, had indeed been a bellhop before being discovered. One of his duties in the Johnny role was touring the country making local appearances touting Philip Morris cigarettes. It was not a bad deal at a twenty thousand dollar annual salary. When discovered in New York in 1933, he was only making fifteen dollars a week as a bellhop. As soon as Johnny arrived at Haag's, our corner drugstore, he passed out sample packs of Philip Morris cigarettes to the assembled adults. I had to watch from the sidelines because I was under age. When asked, he gave his memorable cry and posed for a photo with anyone interested. As Johnny left the drugstore, I wondered if he smoked Philip Morris cigarettes, and if so, had he smoked them for a long time. Was that why he was so short? In those days, the only publicized problem with smoking cigarettes was that it stunted your growth. In later years Johnny gained the reputation of liking big blondes and small yachts.

JOHNNY LEAVING HAAGS DRUG STORE

The only other excitement of note that summer was the appearance of an organ grinder and a real monkey in front of Haag's, where Johnny had performed a few weeks earlier. It didn't take long for word to spread around our neighborhood. The boys and girls assembled with great expectations, as most of us had never seen a real monkey before. Unfortunately Indianapolis didn't have a municipal zoo for another twenty years. However Mary Ellen and I were fortunate to visit the Brookfield Zoo in Chicago during the family's annual treks to the lake place in southern Wisconsin.

Like Johnny of Philip Morris fame, the monkey at Haag's also sported a bright red jacket and black cap. He was trained to walk through the crowd holding a tin cup, looking for coins. The organ grinder in the meantime cranked out popular tunes on his heavy hand organ, which was supported by a stout wooden pole. If someone was kind enough to drop a coin in the cup, the monkey had been trained to tip his cap as a thank you. The organ grinder and monkey never returned to our corner. Perhaps their pickings were slim that day.

Summary

With the end of World War II, the country returned to a peacetime setting requiring a readjustment of civilian priorities. This was particularly difficult for the returning war veterans. *Life Magazine* in late 1945 documented the country's return to normalcy, as they called it. Indianapolis was selected as the All-American City to highlight in a lead nine-page article. One of the article bylines was titled "The People of Indianapolis are Absorbed in Pleasant Trivia." Included in the article was a photograph of the Shortridge High School cheering section rooting for their football team in a city championship game with arch rival Broad Ripple High School. These games attracted as many as seven thousand loyal fans according to the article.

As the 1950s approached, rapid change was in the air for the country and for Indianapolis. The future of the country looked bright since the Great Depression and World War II were behind us. Although the Korean War started in 1950, a feeling of optimism had spread across the country, as jobs were plentiful and the housing boom had already started. Introduced to the market place were many new or improved consumer goods and services that changed our lives forever. With the 1950s came the start of credit cards, dramatic changes in fads and fashions, the ubiquitous television set, home air conditioning, the two-car family, working wives and mothers, the move to the suburbs, the advent of ranch houses, sub-divisions with their cul-de-sacs, and the push for organized children's activities.

My personal life also changed dramatically in 1950 when our family left the old neighborhood for good. My parents moved back to Chicago, where Dad continued to work for Westinghouse Electric Co. for several years before their move to Santa Monica, California, after retirement. For the next two years I boarded with different families on the north side of Indianapolis. During that period I worked full time at Allison Division of General Motors, Plant #5, in Maywood and attended the downtown Indianapolis branch of Indiana University full time as well. In 1952 I left Indianapolis for additional schooling at the I. U. campus in Bloomington, followed by service in the military, employment in the corporate world on the East and West coasts, graduate business degrees from Harvard University and the University of Southern California, marriage and a family of my own.

Conclusions

Growing up in the 1930s and 1940s shaped my beliefs, attitudes, and values, many of which are still with me today, as I view current behavior and events through the cultural prism of that period. As one student of human behavior so rightly put it, "You are what you were at the age of ten."

To understand the dramatic changes in our culture and society over the last 60 plus years, one simple approach is to compare the type of retail shops and entertainment venues that were found in our neighborhoods then with ones we have now and figure out what led to those changes.

My beloved corner shops at 54th and College Avenue are no longer there. The former Haag's Drug Store is now the Jazz Kitchen, featuring live jazz groups and dining, while Silver's Pharmacy is now a military surplus store. The former Krogers Grocery Store and Pure Oil Service Station have been combined into Moe & Johnny's Restaurant. Even Atlas Market, formerly Pedigo's closed its doors and was razed in 2006 after a fifty-year run. The good news is that another specialty grocery store, Fresh Market, has just been built on the site.

Few traces of the old commercial downtown Broad Ripple remain. Gone are the dime stores, hardware stores, auto show rooms, bowling alley, lumber yard, stationery store, auto accessory and sporting goods stores, and most of the grocery stores. Instead, we now have unisex hair stylists, health food stores next to pizza parlors and bagel shops, fast food restaurants next to fitness centers, art galleries next to wine bars, trendy taverns next to coffee houses, high fashion women's clothing boutiques next to hair salons, and Internet cafes next to eBay listing centers.

Most of my former greater Indianapolis bicycle destinations have disappeared, including the Little America amusement park and golf driving range which now features retail shops and low rise office buildings. The site of the former Riverside Amusement Park was cleared and converted into residential dwellings several years ago while the

Uptown Theater was razed and replaced with an Indianapolis Police Department district office which in turn was recently vacated.

The old Monon railroad right-of-way, our favorite place to play as youngsters and where years later I owned the little red caboose on Cornell Avenue, has become a fitness trail. The former Broad Ripple Amusement Park that included a variety of fun rides and the Olympic size outdoor pool has been downsized to a small swimming pool, a bark park for dogs and not much else. The building in Broad Ripple housing School 80, our grade school arch football rival, has been converted into condos, while Shortridge High School has been downgraded to a middle school. However all is not lost; the Riviera Swim Club is still in business and the Indianapolis Motor Speedway has expanded its racing program considerably. Also, my alma mater, the eighty-year-old School 84 is undergoing a twelve million dollar expansion and renovation.

The heart of downtown Indianapolis has also changed remarkably over the years. It has been "sanitized." Gone are most of those ingredients which gave the downtown Indy streetscape its charm, character and a personal uniqueness. Gone are the days when it was fun to go downtown just to window shop. Gone are the hordes of local shoppers dressed up for the occasion in their Sunday best. Gone are the squeals and screeches of the streetcars as their wheels negotiated the tight track turn from Washington Street to Illinois Street. Gone are the movie house marquees with their flashing lights, most of the department stores with their sidewalk level windows filled with the latest fashions and fads, and gone are the transient hotels with the babble of traveling salesmen emanating from their crowded lobbies. Also missing are pawn shop windows crammed with every type of merchandise imaginable, billiard parlors filled with the blue haze of cigarette smoke and the sounds of balls in play, second hand book shops overflowing with stacks of dusty and unwanted books, and the smells of the daily blue plate specials wafting from the doorways of blue collar cafes and bars. Also gone are most of the friendly pan handlers, corner pencil sellers, soapbox orators and evangelists who handed out religious tracts.

One of the saddest changes is the demise of nearby Indiana Avenue where at one time the local colored population had its own vibrant city within a city. Then the Avenue was alive with the hustle and bustle of people on the go and the sounds of live music poured out of the jazz clubs which lined the Avenue. Now Indiana Avenue is just a street name with only the Walker Theater still in business as a reminder of what once upon a time took place there.

My old neighborhood is quiet as well. Gone are the milk and bread route deliverymen in their funny looking little delivery trucks, the summer vegetable vendors hawking their wares from the front sidewalks, the rumble of the large, heavily laden coal and ice trucks as they made their delivery rounds, the friendly knock on the door of the notions salesmen and the credit insurance collector. Gone are the afternoon and early evening newsboys, neighbor ladies chatting over the fence as they hung out their wash, and the noise of the children walking to and from the nearby grade school. Gone are the sounds of the younger children playing kick the can on a warm summer evening; the tinkle of the Good Humor bicycle bell as the young ice cream vendor in his smart looking white uniform made the rounds, the shouts of the older boys passing the football back and forth in the street, and the bevy of boys on bicycles headed to the neighborhood drugstore for a Pepsi or to play the pin ball machine. Gone are families on a warm summer evening strolling over to the nearby drug store for a double dip Tutti-Frutti ice cream cone. Gone are most of the front porch dwellers whose chatter with passersby helped keep the neighborhood closely knit.

However, although much has changed in Indianapolis during the intervening sixty plus years, the important things that make the city special remain intact. It is still a great place to raise a family; it is a caring community and has the neighborliness of a small town along with the conveniences of a large city.

This book began as a way to introduce my children and grand children to my younger life. I hope that they will have a better understanding of those forces that helped shape me as a child and made me who I am today. Perhaps reading my recollections of growing up in Indianapolis will encourage you to think about those fun times you had as a child and pass along those remembrances to your own family members.

Appendix

AUTOGRAPH BOOK SAYINGS

By hook and by crook,
I'll be the first to write in this book.

When you get married, and live across the lake,
Send me a piece of your wedding cake.

I love you little, I love you big,
I love you like a little fat pig.

Mary had a little watch, she swallowed it one day,
Now she takes castor oil to pass the time away.

If I was a little rabbit and had a tail of fluff,
I'd climb into your compact to be your powder puff.

Upon this page I claim a spot,
To write these words, Forget-me-not.

You ask me to write, what shall it be,
Just two little words, Remember Me!

Remember me in all your wishes,
Remember me when you wash the dishes.

Before you are married, it's hearts,
When you are married, it's diamonds,
After you are married, it's clubs,
When you are dead, it's spades.

I never went to college, I never went to school,
But when it comes to loving, I'm an educated fool.

Sailing down the stream of life, I'm a little birch bark canoe,
May it be a pleasant voyage, with only room for two.

When you get married and live down by the river,
Send me a piece of your old man's liver.

A way out yonder, not far off,
A rabbit jumped up and his tail flopped off.

In the parlor there were three, the maid, the parlor lamp and he,
Two is company without a doubt, so the parlor lamp went out.

When you fall down and hurt your knee,
Jump up quick and think of me.

Ashes to ashes, dust to dust,
If you don't go to heaven, to the devil you must.

Yours 'till the ocean wears rubber pants,
To keep its bottom dry.

Remember me far, far off,
Where the woodchucks die with whooping cough.

In this tiny book, I claim this spot,
To write my name, Forget-me-not.

Girls are few, boys are plenty,
Don't marry till you are twenty.

Remember me early, remember me late,
Remember me as an old school mate.

When days are dark, and friends are few,
Think of me and I will you.

Remember me and bear in mind,
That a rooster's tail sticks out behind.

When you see a frog climb a tree,
Pull his tail and think of me.

Down in the valley, carved on a rock,
Just four little words, for-get-me-not.

I pity the baker, I pity the cook,
I pity the one who reads this book.

When you get married and your old lady is cross,
Hang her on the doorknob and tell her you are boss.

Now I lay me down to sleep, I park my flivver on the street,
If it should start before I wake, I pray to God, slam on the brake.

Remember me and bear in mind, a good looking woman is hard to find,
So when you find one hold her tight, and run to the preacher with all your might.